Signature Tastes
of
SPOKANE

This book is a tribute to the sheer determination of Nicole. I know it, she knows it and now the world knows it. Thank you for seeing it to fruition. SWS

Thank you to Steven for bringing me this wonderful project; I am ever grateful for your support and belief that it could be done. Thank you also to my family for helping me complete the book, particularly my mother, Ellen Carlson, and my husband, Marc. NLM

Welcome to Spokane: The Lilac City photography from Muzzy Mount, Discovery Point, and the Washington State University archives.

Welcome to Spokane: The Lilac City information from Wikipedia.

Photography by Nicole L. Manganaro except where noted below.
1. Michael White and Greg Lipsker: Courtesy of Barrister Winery
2. Bon Bon: Jon Jordan
3. Bud Nameck: Panaramio
4. Frank's Diner: Courtesy of Landmark Restaurants
5. Jess Walter: Hannah Assouline
6. Josh Wade: Cameron Glass/CG Photography
Mark Anthony Productions
7. Just American Desserts: Ifong Chen Photography
8. Masselow's: Courtesy of Northern Quest Casino
9. Max at Mirabeau: Courtesy of Mirabeau Park Hotel & Convention Center
10. The Onion: Courtesy of Landmark Restaurants
11. Kristina Mielke-van Löben Sels and James van Löben Sels: Carlton Canary Photography
12. Stephanie and Davide Trezzi: Sean Watson
13. Mary Verner: Courtesy of Mary Verner
14. Stix: Courtesty of Twig's
15. Margaret Croom: Courtesty of Margaret Croom

Front Cover Credit: Photo detail of Spokane Farmers' Market logo. Logo art by Nicole Lund.
Nicole L. Manganaro author photo by Marc Manganaro.
Steven W. Siler author photo by Will Messer

You can find us at www.signaturetastes.com and on Facebook: Signature Tastes of Spokane

Layout by Steven W. Siler

Library of Congress Control Number: 2010914016

Siler, Steven W. and Manganaro, Nicole L.

Signature Tastes of Spokane: Favorite Recipes from our Local Kitchens

ISBN 978-0-9867155-2-5

1. Restaurants-Washington-Spokane-Guidebooks. 2. Cookery-Washington-Spokane

Printed in the United States of America

This book is dedicated to the emergency responders...

From the first frantic call to 9-1-1
To the comforting hands at the E.D.
You give your time...

away from spouses,
away from friends,
away from children,
And yes, even from meals...

To assure all of us:

"Tonight, I will make it better for you
no matter what,
I will watch over you..."

This is not just a cookbook as much as a Culinary Postcard; a celebration of the city itself...about the eateries, fine dining, casual dining, bars, drive-ins, and of course, the people.

The first humans to live in the Spokane area arrived between twelve to eight thousand years ago and were hunter-gatherer societies that lived off the plentiful game in the area. Over time the forests in the area began to thin out

and the Native Americans became more dependent upon roots, berries, and fish. When asked by early white explorers, the tribe said their ancestors came from "up north". The Spokane Falls were the tribe's center of trade and fishing.

Early in the 19th century, the Northwest Fur Company sent two white fur trappers, Jacques Raphael Finlay and Finan McDonald, west of the Rocky Mountains to search for fur. At the confluence of the Little Spokane and Spokane, Finlay and McDonald

built a new fur trading post, which was the first long-term European settlement in Washington state. This trading post known as the Spokane House, or simply "Spokane", was in operation from 1810 to 1826.

Fur bales from the Northwest Fur Company

Joint American–British occupation of Oregon Country, in effect since the Treaty of 1818, eventually led to the Oregon Boundary Dispute as large influxes of American settlers began arriving by the Oregon Trail. The dispute ended with the signing of the Oregon Treaty in 1846 when Great Britain ceded all its claims to lands south of the 49th Parallel, the present day border with Canada.

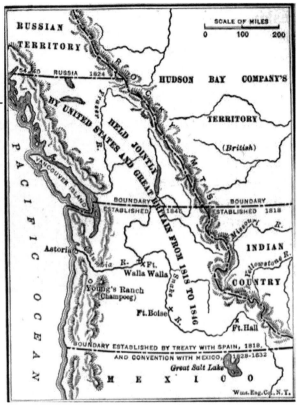

James N. Glover

 James N. Glover and Jasper Matheney, Oregonians passing through the region in 1873, recognized the value of the Spokane River and its falls. They realized the investment potential and bought the claims of 160 acres and the sawmill from J.J. Downing and S.R. Scranton for a total of $4,000. Glover and Matheney knew that the Northern Pacific Railroad Company had received a government charter to build a main line across this northern route. Glover later became known as the "Father of Spokane".

Spokane's growth continued unabated until August 4, 1889, when a fire, now known as The Great Fire, began shortly after 6:00 p.m. and destroyed the city's downtown commercial district. In an effort to impede the fire's growth, firefighters began demolishing buildings with dynamite. The fire continued despite this as the flames leaped over the cleared spaces and created their own firestorm. When volunteer firefighters attempted to quench the

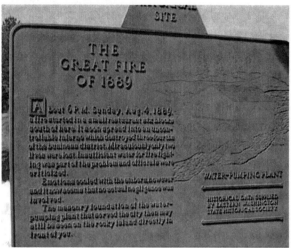

flames, they found their hoses were unusable. Eventually winds died down and the fire exhausted of its own accord. In the fires' aftermath, 32 blocks of Spokane's downtown were destroyed and one person was killed.

Spokane is known as the "Birthplace of Father's Day". Sonora Smart Dodd, often referred to as the "Mother of Father's Day", was 16 years old when her mother died, leaving her father to raise Sonora and her five younger brothers on a remote farm in eastern Washington. In 1909 when Sonora heard a Mother's Day sermon at Central United

Methodist Church in Spokane, she was inspired to propose that fathers receive equal recognition. Sonora suggested her father's birthday, June 5, be established as the day to honor all fathers. However, the pastors wanted more time to prepare, so June 19, 1910 was designated as the first Father's Day.

Spokane hosted the first environmentally themed World's Fair in Expo '74, becoming the smallest city yet to host a World's Fair. Expo '74 also had the distinction of being the first American fair after World War II to be attended by the Soviet Union. This event transformed Spokane's downtown, removing a century of railroad industry that

built the city and reinvented the urban core. After Expo '74, the fairgrounds became the 100-acre Riverfront Park.

Spokane experiences a four-season climate, and is close in proximity to dozens of lakes and rivers for swimming, boating, rafting, and fishing, as well as mountains for skiing, hiking, and biking. Within a short drive from Spokane, visitors can find 76 lakes, 33 golf courses, 16 wineries, 5 ski resorts, 5 major national parks, the Co-

lumbia River Gorge, and the Grand Coulee Dam. Glacier National Park is just 4 hours away from Spokane, and Mt. Rainier National Park and North Cascades National Park are 4 ½ hours away.

Spokane indians along the Spokane
River, 1900's

The Davenport Restaurant
Circa 1900's

RECIPES & RESTAURANTS

NORTHWEST PAELLA

Signature Taste of SPOKANE

2 Tbsp olive oil
2 oz. diced chicken
2 links of chorizo, sliced
½ lb. manila clams
4 oz. lobster meat, diced
8 prawns
¼ C. sliced calamari
1 tsp garlic, minced
1 tsp shallots, minced
1¼ C. diced yellow onion
½ tsp lemon juice
3 Tbsp white wine
½ C. chicken stock
4 C. cooked saffron risotto
¼ C. diced red bell pepper
¼ C. diced tomato
¼ C. sliced asparagus
⅓ C. fresh grated parmesan cheese
pepper, to taste

1. In a large pan, heat the olive oil over high heat until smoking. Add the chicken and chorizo and sear, about 1 minute.

2. Add the clams, lobster, prawns, calamari, garlic, shallots, and onion and sauté until onions are soft, then add the lemon juice, white wine, and chicken stock.

3. Turn heat to medium, add the cooked saffron risotto and simmer for 1 minute.

4. Add the remaining ingredients and stir, cover with a lid for 2 minutes, or until clams open. Serve family style.

AGAVE LATIN BISTRO
830 WEST SPRAGUE AVENUE

"The irony is, we could have gone ahead with the paella, under the new rules. It was free and open to everybody, and we always fed about 3,000 people."
Bob Levy

QUICHE LORRAINE

Tucked away in the unassuming courthouse district, Alpine Bistro welcomes you with aromas of fresh baked pastries and bread that waft in from the adjoining bakery. These aromas, floating through the bistro on the notes of light jazz, set the mood for this quaint escape on Monroe. Whether you are purchasing an artisan loaf of bread or sitting down for a meal, you will feel the warmth and comfort of the Alpine Bistro. Our epicurean offerings consist of European comfort food – predominantly French, German, and Italian cuisine. We also feature a nice selection of local wines and beers.

Crust:
2 ⅔ C. all-purpose flour
1 C. margarine
½ tsp salt
12 Tbsp cold water

Egg Base:
5 eggs + 4 egg yolks
2 C. whole milk
2 C. heavy cream
½ tsp salt
pinch of nutmeg

Filling:
1 C. Gruyère cheese, grated
8 slices of bacon, cooked and crumbled

1. Preheat oven to 375°F.

2. In a large bowl, add the flour, margarine, and salt and mix with a fork until mixture is crumbly.

3. Add water 2 Tbsp at a time and mix until crust is moist and holds together. Use a fork to mix and not your hands so that the crust stays cold.

4. Roll out the crust and a press into a greased 9-inch springform pan so that it covers the bottom and goes about 2 ½ inches up the side. Pierce crust all over with fork to prevent bubbling.

5. Cut a 12x12-inch piece of parchment paper and cover the crust. Fill the springform pan with pie weights reaching up to the top of crust to keep it from curling down during baking. Bake crust for 15 minutes.

6. In a bowl, mix together all the ingredients for the egg base.

7. Sprinkle the Gruyère and bacon into the bottom of the baked crust and then pour in the egg base and bake for 45–60 minutes, or until a knife comes out clean when inserted in the middle of the quiche.

ALPINE BISTRO & BAKERY CO.
810 NORTH MONROE STREET

"Nothing makes us happier than to have our customers feel like they are part of our Alpine family."
Carl, Nicole, Kyle, Doug, Alex Burgi, and our entire Alpine staff

RACK OF LAMB WITH POMEGRANATE-PORT GASTRIQUE

Signature Tastes of SPOKANE

Rosemary Black-Pepper Crust:
4 Tbsp fresh rosemary leaves
1½ Tbsp whole black peppercorns
3-4 whole garlic cloves
olive oil

Pomegranate-Port Gastrique:
½ 750 ml bottle California ruby Port, (approximately 1½ C.)
1 ¾ C. granulated sugar
¼ C. corn starch slurry (mix equal parts corn starch and water until smooth)
3 oz. pomegranate molasses (found in specialty food stores)
canola oil

2 (8-bone, 14-16 oz.) New Zealand lamb racks, trimmed and Frenched, cut into 4 bone sections

Rosemary Black-Pepper Crust:
1. In a food processor equipped with a chopping blade, pulse together the rosemary, black peppercorns, and garlic until finely chopped. With the motor running, drizzle olive oil through the top in a small stream until ingredients just come together. (Do not add too much oil.) Liberally coat the lamb racks with the paste, avoiding the bones. Place in a shallow pan, loosely cover, and refrigerate for 2-24 hours.

Pomegranate-Port Gastrique:
1. In a non-reactive sauce pan, reduce port by half over medium heat. Add pomegranate molasses and sugar and bring to a boil, stirring occasionally until the sugar melts. Add the corn starch slurry and continue to cook until the gastrique is thick enough to coat the back of a spoon. Keep warm.

Lamb:
1. Preheat oven to 350°F.
2. In an oven-safe pan, heat 1-2 Tbsp of canola oil over medium-high heat and sear the lamb racks, bone side down, until well browned, about 3-4 minutes.
3. Turn the racks over and place the pan in the oven to finish, approximately 10 minutes for medium rare.
4. Remove the pan from the oven, cover racks loosely with foil, and let rest 5-7 minutes.
5. Slice racks between the bones, divide among two plates, and drizzle with pomegranate-port gastrique. Serve with horseradish Yukon Gold mashed potatoes and grilled asparagus.

AMBROSIA BISTRO & WINE BAR
9211 EAST MONTGOMERY AVENUE

"Come taste Ambrosia for yourself!"
Jeremiah Timmons
Executive Chef

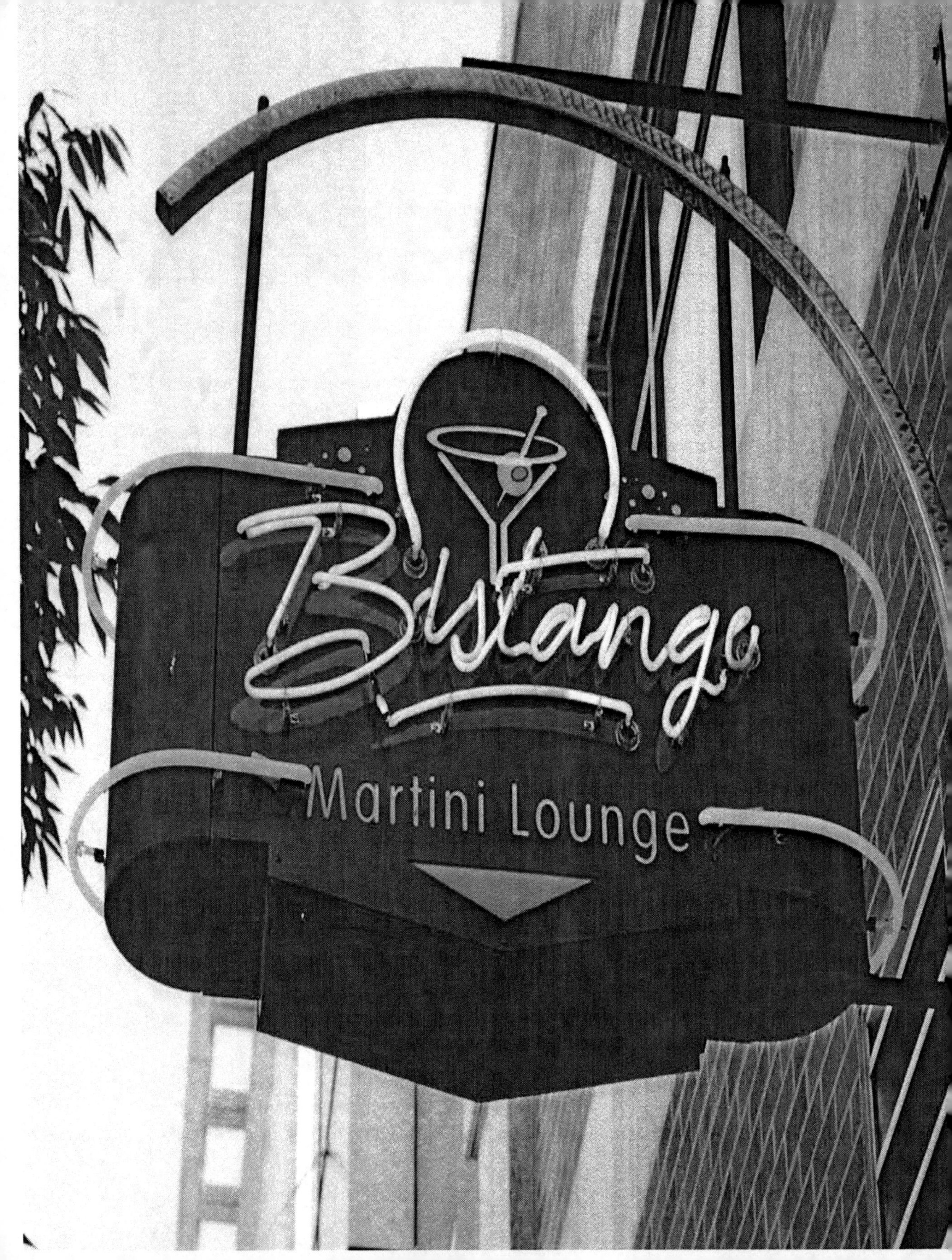
Bistango
Martini Lounge

STRAWBERRY BASIL MARTINI

Bistango is an upscale cocktail lounge conveniently located in the heart of downtown Spokane. It is the perfect place to begin or end your evening, so join us after work, for business meetings, or as a break from shopping. Be sure to sample our food menu which is full of tasty flavors that blend perfectly with cocktails.

Sweet and Sour Mix:
1 C. granulated sugar
1 C. water
¼ C. fresh squeezed lemon juice
¼ C. fresh squeezed lime juice

Strawberry Basil Martini:
2 fresh strawberries, quartered, plus more for garnish
2-4 fresh basil leaves
3 oz. premium vodka
1 ½ oz. sweet and sour mix
1 oz. white grapefruit juice
ice

Sweet and Sour Mix:
1. Make the simple syrup first by combining the sugar and water in a small sauce pan, bring to a simmer, stirring until sugar is dissolved, about 3 minutes. Cool completely.

2. Mix 1/4 C. fresh lime juice and 1/4 C. fresh lemon juice with 1/2 C. of the simple syrup to make the sweet and sour mix.

Strawberry Basil Martini:
1. Place ice, strawberries, and basil in a cocktail shaker and muddle well.

2. Add the vodka, sweet and sour mix, and white grapefruit juice, shake well, and strain into a chilled martini glass. Garnish with a whole strawberry on the edge of the glass.

BISTANGO MARTINI LOUNGE
108 NORTH POST STREET

"Get in touch with your senses—let Bistango take you beyond the martini and into the experience...."
Reema Shaver, Owner

BETSIE'S SMILE

The Blue Spark is a legendary local hot spot with twenty-six tap handles, great specialty cocktails, and it is the best place for live bands, pub trivia, and tons of other events. Funky décor provides a great atmosphere along with our fantastic service and never ending drink specials. We guarantee that you will always have a good time at The Spark!

Signature Tastes of SPOKANE

1½ oz. Cruzan
mango rum

1½ oz. Stoli peach
flavored vodka

½ oz. lemonade

½ oz. orange juice

splash of cranberry juice

1. Fill a cocktail shaker with ice, add the rum, vodka, lemonade, and orange juice, shake well and strain into a martini glass. Top with a splash of cranberry juice.

THE BLUE SPARK
15 SOUTH HOWARD STREET

"A woman drove me to drink and I didn't even have the decency to thank her"
W.C. Fields

TWENTY-FIRST CENTURY COCKTAIL

Bon Bon is a sweet and sassy classic cocktail joint located on the corner of Monroe Street and Garland Avenue, attached to the Garland Theater. The lovely staff has been studying vintage recipes from dusty old cocktail books unearthing cocktails that will knock your socks off! A refreshing libation to enjoy under the twinkling lights of the marquee would be the Twenty-first Century Cocktail.

Signature Tastes of SPOKANE

splash of absinthe

2 oz. tequila

¾ oz. crème de cacao

¾ oz. fresh squeezed lemon juice

1. Pour a splash of absinthe into a martini glass and swirl to coat the inside of the glass. Spill out the remainder of the absinthe so that it leaves only a small puddle in the bottom of the glass.

2. Combine tequila, crème de cacao, and lemon juice in a cocktail shaker filled with ice. Shake well and strain into the absinthe coated glass.

BON BON

926 WEST GARLAND AVENUE

"The problem with the world is that everyone is a few drinks behind."
Humphrey Bogart

At Cake, we take pride in combining fresh, quality ingredients to create desserts that are lighter, less sweet, and more flavorful for today's appetites. Dedicated to offering a variety of unique and fresh specialties, we always make our desserts with the care and attention fine food requires.

Crust:
3 C. all-purpose flour
1 C. confectioners' sugar,
plus more for dusting
¼ tsp salt
1½ C. unsalted butter,
cold, cubed

Lemon Filling:
8 large eggs
4 C. granulated sugar
⅔ C. all-purpose flour
1½ C. freshly squeezed
lemon juice
1 Tbsp lemon zest

1. Preheat oven to 350°F.

2. To make the crust, whisk together 3 C. flour, confectioners' sugar, and salt in a large bowl.

3. Using a pastry blender, cut in the butter until the pieces are the size of peas.

4. Press mixture into the bottom of an ungreased 10x15-inch rimmed baking pan and bake 20–30 minutes, until golden. Cool.

5. Meanwhile, make the filling. In a medium bowl, whisk together the eggs, sugar, and ⅔ C. flour until just combined.

6. Whisk in the lemon juice and zest until combined and pour filling onto cooled crust.

7. Return pan to oven and bake for 30 minutes, rotating pan halfway through, until set. Cool completely.

8. Dust with confectioners' sugar and cut into bars.

4237 SOUTH CHENEY SPOKANE ROAD

CAKE

"Dear Bakery, I have been thinking of you. Your liberation is bound up in the labor of others. Be kind to them dear bakery. A thousand invisible threads connect you to those that dream of you, and through them flows commitment, patience, and life…"
E. E. Hale

For the most authentic Mexican food you can find anywhere we invite you to come to Casa de Oro. From the moment you walk in you will be treated like family. Our knowledgeable staff will make sure you are completely satisfied with our quality food and service.

Chicken and Stock:
8 chicken legs with thighs, skin on (or 1 whole chicken, cut up)
1 clove of garlic
½ of 1 onion, peeled
1 Tbsp fresh oregano, chopped (1 tsp dried)
6 C. of water
2 tsp salt

Mole Sauce:
1 (16-oz.) can whole tomatoes, drained
1 chipotle chile in adobo
5 Tbsp oil, divided
2 dried ancho chiles, deseeded, sliced
2 dried pasilla chiles, deseeded, sliced
2 dried mulato chiles, deseeded, sliced
½ of 1 onion, peeled, cut into wedges
2 whole garlic cloves
2 oz. almonds, blanched
2 oz. unsalted roasted peanuts
4 whole cloves
2 black peppercorns
1 cinnamon stick, about 2-cm long
1 oz. raisins
1 oz. unsweetened baking chocolate
1 tsp sugar
1 oz. toasted sesame seeds
salt, to taste
corn tortillas

Chicken and Stock:
1. Place chicken, garlic, onion, oregano, water, and salt in a large pot and bring to a boil. Cover and simmer until chicken is tender, about 40 minutes. Remove the chicken then strain and reserve the stock.

Mole Sauce:
1. Purée chipotle chile and tomatoes in a blender, pour into a bowl, and set aside.
2. Heat 2 Tbsp of oil in a skillet over medium heat, add the ancho, pasilla, and mulato chiles and sauté for 2 minutes. Leave oil in the skillet and transfer chiles to a bowl, add hot water, and soak for 30 minutes. Drain, then purée, pour into a bowl, and set aside.
3. Using the same oil in the skillet, sauté the onion and garlic for 2–3 minutes over medium heat. Transfer to the blender.
4. Add almonds to the skillet and sauté for 5 minutes. Add to the blender.
5. Add peanuts, cloves, peppercorns, and cinnamon stick to the skillet and sauté for 3 minutes. Add to the blender.
6. Add the raisins to the blender and purée all the ingredients together.

Finish the Mole:
1. Heat 3 Tbsp of oil in a large pot over medium-high heat, add all of the purées and bring to a boil. Cook for 5 minutes, stirring often. Add the chocolate and sugar and stir.
2. Add 3 C. of reserved chicken stock and bring to a boil, cover, reduce heat, and simmer for 20 minutes. Add more stock if sauce is too thick.
3. Add the chicken to the sauce, cover, and cook over medium heat until chicken is hot.
4. Sprinkle the finished dish with sesame seeds and serve with corn tortillas.

CASA DE ORO
4111 NORTH DIVISION STREET

"The one thing our customers comment on the most is how fresh our food tastes. The reason for that is very simple—our owner Enrique Torres hand selects all of the ingredients that go into our food."
Eva Torres, Co-owner

BEEF STROGANOFF

Located in the cellar of the historic Montvale Hotel, Catacombs Pub combines great food with old-world architecture, making for an unforgettably unique dining experience. The exposed stone, solid-oak beams, (each weighing 2,800 pounds!) and warm brick hearth are features modeled after the finest German and Viennese pubs. The food reflects the cuisine styles from central Europe including Austria, Germany, Hungary, and Italy.

½ C. Worcestershire sauce
1 (3-lb.) beef shoulder, trimmed of excess fat, cut into 1-inch cubes
⅛ C. + ¼ C. all-purpose flour, divided
1 Tbsp olive oil
½ C. yellow onion, chopped
½ C. full-bodied red wine
⅔ C. mixed mushrooms, sliced (such as oyster, chanterelle, and shiitake)
10 large crimini mushrooms, sliced
4 C. hot water
1 Tbsp beef base (such as Minor's brand)
1 tsp spice blend (recipe follows)
½ C. unsalted butter
4–5 Tbsp sour cream

Spice Blend:
1 tsp nutmeg
2 tsp English mustard powder
½ tsp ground cloves
½ tsp freshly ground pepper

1. Preheat oven to 425°F.
2. Heat Worcestershire sauce in a small sauté pan over medium-high until liquid is reduced by half, approximately 5–7 minutes.
3. Dredge beef cubes in 1/8 C. of the flour.
4. Pour the olive oil into a large casserole dish and add the beef chunks and chopped onions and place uncovered in the oven to brown the meat, approximately 10 minutes.
5. When beef is browned, remove casserole from the oven and stir in the wine and the mushrooms.
6. Whisk together the hot water, 1 Tbsp of the beef base, and 1 tsp of the spice blend. Pour mixture over the beef and stir well.
7. Add the Worcestershire reduction to the beef and stir well.
8. Cover casserole dish with foil and place in the oven for 45 minutes.
9. Meanwhile, make a roux by melting the butter in sauté pan over medium heat. Whisking constantly, slowly add remaining ¼ C. of flour to butter and cook the roux approximately 3 minutes. When the beef is done, uncover and stir in the roux until beef is well coated.
10. Re-cover casserole and place in the oven for an additional 45 minutes.
11. Stir in 4–5 Tbsp of sour cream, season to taste, and serve the stroganoff over egg noodles.

"I love to look around a busy kitchen—the heat and pressure are almost unbearable—and the cooks, in perfect synchronization, make it all look effortless."
Tug Warrick, Head Chef

Carrot-Cake Cupcakes

Celebrations Bakery is located in the quaint Garland District located in North Spokane where you'll find folks strolling along Garland Avenue, shopping at the Corner Cottage, eating at the historic Milk Bottle, or taking in a movie at the Garland Theater. Our cupcakery is known for its vast variety of delectable flavors like maple bacon, banana split, peanut butter cup, and our tempting red velvet with cream cheese frosting, as well as our happy hour – where else can you get over fifteen different flavors of cupcakes for one dollar the entire hour?

Cupcakes:
2 eggs
1 ⅛ C. granulated sugar
⅓ C. brown sugar, packed
½ C. vegetable oil
1 tsp vanilla extract
1¾ C. shredded carrots
½ C. crushed pineapple, drained well
1½ C. all-purpose flour
1¼ tsp baking soda
½ tsp salt
2 tsp cinnamon
¼ tsp ground ginger
¾ tsp ground nutmeg
1 C. finely chopped walnuts (optional)

Cream Cheese Frosting:
1 (8-oz.) package of cream cheese, softened
½ C. unsalted butter, softened
1 tsp vanilla extract
3 C. confectioners' sugar

Cupcakes:
1. Preheat oven to 350°F.
2. Lightly grease a 12-cup muffin tin.
3. Using a mixer, beat together the eggs and sugars in a bowl.
4. Mix in the oil and vanilla.
5. Fold in the carrots and pineapple.
6. In a separate bowl, mix together the flour, baking soda, salt, cinnamon, ginger, and nutmeg.
7. Add flour mixture into the wet carrot mixture and stir until moist.
8. Fold in walnuts (optional).
9. Pour batter into muffin tins and bake cupcakes for 25 minutes or until a toothpick inserted into the center comes out clean. Cool completely on wire racks before frosting.

Cream Cheese Frosting:
1. Beat the cream cheese, butter, and vanilla extract together with a mixer set over high speed until light and fluffy.
2. Add the confectioners' sugar and beat at medium speed until frosting is smooth.
3. Spread or pipe the frosting onto the cooled cupcakes.

Note: The frosted cupcakes can be garnished with additional chopped walnuts or cinnamon sugar, if desired.

Celebrations Bakery
713 West Garland Avenue

"We absolutely love how many smiles a cupcake will bring and we look forward to really getting to know each and every customer."
Christina Levinson, Owner

The CHALET RESTAURANT

Fine
Family
Dining

SLICKROCK
SALON G AND
Edward

WESTERN BENNY

Signature Tastes of SPOKANE

2 sausage patties

2 eggs

2 qt. water

white vinegar

1 English muffin, split and toasted

2 Tbsp Campbell's White Cream Sauce, or more to taste

2 slices of cheddar cheese

1. Cook the sausage patties in a pan until browned and heated through.

2. To poach the eggs, combine 2 qt. of water with a splash of white vinegar in a wide sauce pan and bring to a simmer. Break 1 egg into a small bowl and slide egg into water. Repeat with remaining egg, spacing them evenly in sauce pan, and poach at a bare simmer until whites are firm and yolks are still runny, 2–3 minutes. Transfer eggs to paper towels using a slotted spoon.

3. Place one sausage patty on each muffin half, then add the poached egg, spoon cream sauce over the egg, and top with sliced cheddar cheese. Serve with a side of hash browns.

THE CHALET RESTAURANT
2918 SOUTH GRAND BOULEVARD

Lemuel Benedict, a retired Wall Street stock broker, claimed that he had wandered into the Waldorf Hotel in 1894 and, hoping to find a cure for his morning hangover, ordered "buttered toast, poached eggs, crisp bacon, and a hooker of hollandaise." Oscar Tschirky, the famed maître d'hôtel, was so impressed with the dish that he put it on the breakfast and luncheon menus but substituted ham for the bacon and a toasted English muffin for the toast.

BLUEBERRY MUFFIN FRENCH TOAST

Welcome to Chaps! The idea for Chaps was first conceived when I was a little cowgirl in Montana, where I was nurtured, encouraged, and championed by my two loving grandparents. They remain very much alive today within the decor, the food, and hopefully, the warmth I remember so vividly. I designed, built, and furnished the café with materials, art, and objects from my family's homestead in order to evoke special meaning and memories. I am proud to serve you in the same aprons my grandmother wore while caring for her own family. I hope your time at Chaps brings as much pleasure to you as I am having in sharing it!

Blueberry Muffin French Toast:
2½ C. unsalted butter
3 C. sugar
5 whole eggs
1 tsp vanilla extract
6¼ C. all-purpose flour
1 Tbsp + 1 tsp baking powder
½ tsp salt
1½ C. fresh blueberries

Cream Cheese Frosting:
3 (8-oz.) packages of cream cheese, softened
1½ C. confectioners' sugar
1 C. fresh blueberries
½ tsp vanilla extract
¼ tsp salt

1. Preheat oven to 350°F.

2. Using a stand mixer, cream the butter and sugar together on high speed until light and fluffy.

3. Add the eggs and vanilla and mix on medium speed until incorporated. Scrape down sides of the bowl.

4. Add the flour, baking powder, and salt and mix until well combined.

5. Add the blueberries and mix briefly on low speed.

6. Spread mixture into a greased 9x12-inch pan and bake for 1 hour, or until a toothpick inserted in the center comes out clean.

7. Meanwhile, make the cream cheese frosting by whipping all the ingredients together in a stand mixer set on high speed.

8. To serve, cut blueberry muffin French toast into squares and serve with whipped cream cheese frosting on top.

4235 SOUTH CHENEY SPOKANE ROAD

CHAPS

"Dreams do come true!"
Celeste Shaw
Owner and Chef

PULLED PORK SANDWICH

Charley's Grill is synonymous with great food and spirits. It is a place where old friends get together and new friends are made daily! Join us for happy hour Monday through Saturday from 4–7 pm. We have karaoke every Saturday night – come and hear the best karaoke in Spokane. If you need an event catered Charley's Catering Company offers full service catering at the location of your choice. We can help you plan, stage, and coordinate all aspects of your event.

Dry Rub:
1 C. paprika
½ C. onion powder
2 Tbsp dried oregano
1 Tbsp dried thyme
1 Tbsp cumin
1 Tbsp chili powder
1 Tbsp red chili flakes

Pork Roast:
1 (10-lb.) bone-in pork shoulder roast (Boston butt)
8 C. apple juice
¼ C. vinegar
barbeque sauce

1. Combine all the dry rub spices together in a small bowl. Pat the roast dry with paper towels and rub spices all over the pork roast, wrap the roast in plastic wrap, then wrap in foil and chill overnight (or at least 3 hours) in the refrigerator.

2. Preheat oven to 300°F.

3. Unwrap the pork roast and place in a large roasting pan. Add the apple juice and vinegar and cover the roast loosely with foil. Roast in the oven for 6–8 hours, or until the meat pulls away from the bone.

4. Lay the roast out on a large cutting board and shred the meat using two forks and place meat in a large bowl. Add your favorite barbeque sauce to the meat and mix well. Serve the pulled pork on your favorite roll or bun.

CHARLEY'S GRILL & SPIRITS
801 NORTH MONROE STREET

"Thank you for your patronage! We are locally owned and have been serving the neighborhood for over thirty years!"
Shirley Williams, Owner

PEACH COBBLER

Owner and Chef Bob Hemphill has brought the taste of Texas to Spokane, Washington. Chicken-n-More is recognized as a down home place that serves up the best fried chicken, moist and meaty pork spare ribs, and farm-raised catfish from Alabama.

Signature Tastes of SPOKANE

7 C. granulated sugar	**1.** Preheat oven to 350°F.
2 Tbsp cinnamon	**2.** Mix the sugar and cinnamon together in a bowl.
5 C. self-rising flour	**3.** Mix ⅛ C. of sugar and cinnamon mixture with the flour then stir in the milk.
5 C. milk	
1 (#10-can, 106 oz.) sliced peaches, drained	**4.** Place the peaches in a large bowl and add the vanilla extract and lemon juice and stir well. Add the remaining sugar and cinnamon mixture to the peaches and stir.
1 Tbsp vanilla extract	
2 Tbsp lemon juice	**5.** Pour the melted butter into a large pan and add the peaches and stir to combine.
1 C. unsalted butter, melted	**6.** Pour the flour and milk mixture evenly over the top of the peaches and bake for 1 hour and 20 minutes, or until top is golden brown.

CHICKEN-N-MORE
414 WEST SPRAGUE AVENUE

"Come enjoy our southern hospitality and relaxing atmosphere while savoring the best southern-style food in the Northwest."
Bob Hemphill, Owner and Chef

CITRUS-LACED HOT CHOCOLATE

Chocolate Apothecary is a destination gourmet chocolate, gelato, and coffee shop. We dispense chocolate with knowledge and abandon! Come and enjoy our decadent selection. Drinking chocolates are our specialty and our staff is delighted to help you choose the correct tonic. Celebrate all the seasons of life with us!

Citrus Zest:
1 lemon, orange, or lime

Citrus-Zest Whipped Cream:
½ C. heavy cream
1 Tbsp confectioners' sugar
reserved fine citrus zest

Hot Chocolate:
4 C. whole milk (may substitute soy)
reserved citrus zest strips
8 oz. premium semisweet chocolate

Citrus Zest:
1. Using a paring knife or zester tool, peel ¾ of the citrus fruit's zest into thin strips, being careful not to include the bitter white pith layer. Set aside.
2. Zest the remaining ¼ of the peel with the smallest holes on a box grater to create fine shreds. Reserve the fine citrus zest for the whipped cream.

Citrus-Zest Whipped Cream:
1. In a bowl, whip the heavy cream and confectioners' sugar together with a mixer set on high speed until light and fluffy. Stir in the fine citrus zest and keep chilled until ready to use.

Hot Chocolate:
1. In a sauce pan, combine the milk and citrus-zest strips and bring to a simmer over medium heat. Turn down the heat and let mixture simmer gently for about 5 minutes. Do not boil. Using a slotted spoon, remove the citrus-zest strips from the milk and discard.
2. Add the chocolate and stir constantly until melted.
3. Pour the hot chocolate into mugs and top each with the citrus-zest whipped cream and serve.

Note: For a lovely light drink, use a hand-held blender or milk frother to blend the hot chocolate just before serving.

CHOCOLATE APOTHECARY
621 WEST MALLON AVENUE

"I have the best job in the world! Every day at the shop I am witness to the fact that people are happier for having enjoyed the most pleasant medicine on the planet—Chocolate!"
Susan Davis, Owner

SEAFOOD CHOPHOUSE
C.I. Shenanigans
BREWERY

PAN SEARED SCALLOPS WITH PURPLE POTATO HASH

Purple Potato Hash:
1 lb. purple Peruvian potatoes
2 oz. canola oil
4 oz. diced chorizo
kosher salt
freshly-ground black pepper

Roasted-Poblano Beurre Blanc:
1 C. white wine
juice of 1 lemon
1 small shallot, chopped
2 garlic cloves, chopped
1 C. heavy cream
1 C. unsalted butter, chilled and cubed
kosher salt
1 poblano chile, roasted, peeled, de-seeded, and minced

Scallops:
1 lb. fresh or frozen sea scallops
kosher salt
black pepper
2 Tbsp canola oil

Purple Potato Hash:
1. Peel the potatoes, cut into 1-inch dice. Place potatoes in a pot and fill with water covering potatoes by 1 inch, bring potatoes to a simmer, uncovered, and cook until fork tender, about 15 minutes. Set aside and cool.
2. In a large sauté pan heat the oil over medium-high heat, add diced chorizo and cook until browned. Add reserved potatoes and sauté until potatoes are hot. Season to taste with kosher salt and black pepper.

Roasted-Poblano Beurre Blanc:
1. Preheat oven to 500°F and roast the poblano chile until the skin is black. Place in a plastic bag and after it has cooled, peel off the skin. Remove the seeds and mince.
2. Place wine, lemon juice, shallot, and garlic in medium sauce pan and bring to a boil over medium-high heat. Reduce liquid until almost dry, approximately 5 minutes. Add the heavy cream and reduce by half, approximately 5 minutes.
3. Remove the sauce pan from heat, whisk in the chilled butter slowly. Be careful not to let the sauce separate. Whisk in the minced poblano chile. Season to taste with kosher salt.

Scallops:
1. In a large sauté pan, heat the oil over medium-high heat. Pat scallops dry with a paper towel and season with salt and pepper. When the oil starts to smoke, add scallops and cook until golden brown, about 3 minutes. Turn scallops and cook for about 2 minutes more until golden.
2. To finish the dish place a portion of purple potato hash in the center of each plate. Spoon the roasted-poblano beurre blanc onto the plate around the potatoes. Arrange the scallops on each plate and serve.

C. I. SHENANIGANS
332 NORTH SPOKANE FALLS COURT

A SPOKANE CLASSIC

Clinkerdagger

SINCE 1974

STEAK, CHOP & FISH HOUSE

BROADWAY PEA SALAD

Clinkerdagger has a thirty-seven-year tradition of dining excellence in Spokane. Overlooking the majestic Spokane River and city skyline, Clinkerdagger is the perfect setting for special occasions or entertaining guests. With award-winning service and incredible cuisine our staff invites you to indulge yourself for a truly memorable dining experience.

½ C. mayonnaise

½ C. sour cream

1 tsp white pepper

1 tsp kosher salt

4 oz. snow peas, bud and strings removed

3½ lbs. frozen baby peas, thawed*

5 oz. water chestnuts, sliced

3 oz. bacon, cooked crisp, chopped

2 ½ oz. red onion, ¼-inch dice

1. To make the dressing, blend together mayonnaise, sour cream, white pepper, and salt.

2. Combine snow peas, baby peas, water chestnuts, bacon, and red onions with dressing until ingredients are well coated.

3. Refrigerate at least 24 hours before serving. Stir twice during refrigeration to redistribute dressing.

*Note: Peas must be naturally thawed. Slow thawing under refrigeration is best. Place thawed peas on paper-towel lined pans and let stand at room temperature for 30 minutes to purge the excess moisture from the peas. If peas are not thoroughly thawed or not properly drained, they will dilute the dressing.

CLINKERDAGGER
621 WEST MALLON AVENUE

"Clinkerdagger always goes the extra step in taking care of our guests; you can see it whether you join us for a business lunch or family dinner. We're a Spokane original and we look forward to remaining a part of the community for years to come."
Bob Aldred, Head Chef

CHICKEN FRIED STEAK

Signature Tastes of SPOKANE

Owners Drew and Kim Baker have created a hip, relaxed atmosphere in this breakfast and lunch spot located in the Spokane Valley. We offer a huge variety of traditional choices as well as our own special offerings that we are quite proud of! Compliment your meal with one of our specialty coffees or hot chocolate or your favorite beer or wine. Our batters are made from scratch, we make cinnamon rolls every morning, and you can even get a cheeseburger at 6:30 am!

1 (8-10 oz.) petite sirloin steak

1¼ C. plain bread crumbs

1 Tbsp Montreal steak seasoning

liquid pasteurized eggs

oil for frying

1. In a small bowl, mix the Montreal steak seasoning with the bread crumbs and set aside.

2. Place the sirloin steak in another bowl and pour enough liquid eggs over the steak so that every part of the steak is submerged. Lift steak out, shake off excess, and then dip in bread crumb mixture. Firmly press bread crumbs into steak with your hands and wrap the steak in plastic wrap and refrigerate overnight.

3. In a frying pan, heat oil to 350°F and remove steak from plastic wrap. Fry steak 4–5 minutes until steak is golden brown. Serve steak with a ladle of homemade gravy, fresh cut cottage fries, eggs, and buttered toast with homemade strawberry jam.

COTTAGE CAFÉ

6902 EAST APPLEWAY BOULEVARD

"Only a rank degenerate would drive 1,500 miles across Texas without eating a chicken-fried steak."
Larry McMurtry, **In a Narrow Grave**

Signature Tastes of SPOKANE

The "G" in Crazy G's is Gary Swiss. At the ripe old age of fifty-six, Gary's thirty-year-old dream finally came true. In 2008 Gary retired from engineering and moved his wife Chris to Spokane so she could be close to family. Gary began working on several ideas and inventions that had plagued him for years, and the one that kept creeping back into his mind was his dream of opening a burger joint. Everyone said he was crazy — hence the name, Crazy G's. It was very important to Gary and Chris that they had a restaurant that they would want to come to — one that treated their customers like friends and family. But most of all, they want to make sure you don't go away hungry or that you had to sell your first born to eat at Crazy G's!

2 Tbsp unsalted butter	**1.** On a griddle or flat pan melt butter over medium heat. Add the onions and green peppers and sauté until the peppers are soft and the onions are translucent. Remove from heat, set aside.
¼ C. white sweet onion, sliced	
¼ C. green pepper, sliced	**2.** Place the beef on the griddle, separating the slices, season with salt, pepper, and garlic powder to taste. When the beef is almost cooked, add the peppers and the onions and mix well.
6 oz. thinly sliced Angus beef (from a sirloin ball tip roast)	
salt and pepper, to taste	**3.** Place the provolone cheese on top, cover with a lid, and let it steam to melt the cheese.
garlic powder, to taste	
2 slices provolone cheese	**4.** Spoon everything into a pub roll, cut in half, and enjoy.
1 (8-inch) pub roll	

CRAZY G'S
821 NORTH DIVISION STREET

"We hope you enjoy our homestyle burgers, philly's, and dogs. The idea may be thirty-years-old but the food is made fresh just for you."
Gary and Chris Swiss, Owners

Pork Medallions with Apple Brandy Sauce

Signature Tastes of SPOKANE

1 (1-lb.) boneless pork tenderloin

Calgary steak seasoning

flour for coating

clarified butter

8 oz. heavy cream

4 oz. apple juice

2 oz. brandy

2–3 Tbsp sugar

1 red delicious apple, sliced thinly into 12 pieces

crushed walnuts

1. Trim fat and silver from the pork tenderloin and cut into 2½ oz. medallions. Season the pork lightly with Calgary steak seasoning then lightly coat with flour. Heat the clarified butter in a sauté pan over medium heat, add the pork medallions, and heat slowly until temperature of the medallions reaches 150°F.

2. Meanwhile, make the apple brandy sauce. In a small bowl, combine the heavy cream, apple juice, brandy, and sugar to taste. Pour the ingredients into a separate sauté pan and reduce slowly over medium heat until thickened. When sauce is almost thickened add the apple slices.

3. Top the cooked pork medallions with the apple brandy sauce and sprinkle the crushed walnuts over top.

DAS STEIN HAUS
1812 WEST FRANCIS AVENUE

"Unique dishes from our homeland will be a culinary adventure for you, your family, and friends."
George Weimer, Owner

Located in the cherished Audubon Park neighborhood, The Downriver Grill offers an elegant and delicious dining experience. Family owned and operated since 2003, this award-winning restaurant serves the best in fresh and local food, as well as exquisite local Washington wines, hand-crafted cocktails, and microbrews. Voted Spokane's "Best New Restaurant" by The Inlander Reader's Poll, and by the Washington Restaurant Association, The Downriver Grill is a favorite among locals. Come enjoy seasonal menu specials, flavorful sauces made from scratch, delicious sandwiches, the best in fresh seafood and steaks, and decadent housemade desserts.

Puttanesca Sauce:
5 oz. Sonnenberg's sausage, casings removed, crumbled
½ C. Northern Lights Cream Ale beer
1½ tsp olive oil
2 large anchovy fillets
pinch of chili flakes
1 tsp minced garlic
½ tsp minced shallots
pinch of dried basil
¼ C. Kalamata olives, pitted
¾ tsp capers
pinch of dried rosemary
pinch of dried basil
¼ C. red wine
5 oz. marinara sauce
salt and pepper, to taste
10 oz. cooked linguini

Garnish:
freshly grated parmesan cheese
chopped basil

1. Place the sausage and the beer in a small sauté pan and heat over medium heat until the sausage is cooked through. Drain excess liquid.

2. Add the olive oil to a medium sauté pan and heat the oil over medium-high heat. Once the oil is very hot, but not smoking, add the anchovies and chili flakes. Stir to dissolve the anchovies. Add the garlic and shallots and cook for 2 minutes. Add the cooked sausage, olives, capers, and a pinch of dried rosemary and dried basil and stir well.

3. Deglaze the pan with the red wine and reduce liquid by half, then add the marinara sauce. Season to taste with salt and pepper.

4. Toss the cooked linguini with the puttanesca sauce, divide pasta among two plates, and garnish with freshly grated parmesan cheese and chopped basil.

DOWNRIVER GRILL
3315 WEST NORTHWEST BLVD

"We are excited about partnering with other great local companies and we are thrilled to be a part of the culinary culture in Spokane!"
Aaron Sweatt, General Manager

DRY FLY COCKTAILS

Signature Tastes of SPOKANE

Dry Fly Distilling is a craft distillery in Spokane, Washington. We produce craft-distilled vodka, gin, and whiskey using only locally grown grains and botanicals. Our still, manufactured in Goppingen, Germany, is a Christian Carl pot still with multiple rectification columns. It has a 450-liter capacity and we expect an annual output of approximately 3,500 cases of 12/750 mL bottles. Dry Fly is owned and operated by Don Poffenroth and Kent Fleischmann. Here are a few simple ideas for delicious Dry Fly cocktails.

Dry Fly Apple Martini:
3 oz. Dry Fly gin
¼-inch cubed apple

Dry Fly Apple Martini:
1. Shake Dry Fly gin with ice in a cocktail shaker, strain into a cocktail glass, and garnish with apple cube.

PMD:
2 oz. Dry Fly vodka
cranberry juice

PMD:
1. Fill a glass with ice and add Dry Fly vodka and a splash of cranberry juice.

Sweet Retreat:
2 oz. Dry Fly wheat
whiskey
ginger ale

Sweet Retreat:
1. Fill a glass with ice and add Dry Fly wheat whiskey and a splash of ginger ale.

Driftboat:
2 oz. Dry Fly Bourbon
101
3-4 fresh peach slices

Driftboat:
1. Muddle fresh peach slices in a cocktail shaker with ice, add Dry Fly Bourbon and shake well, strain into a cocktail glass.

DRY FLY DISTILLING
1003 EAST TRENT AVENUE

"Always carry a flagon of whiskey in case of snakebite and furthermore always carry a small snake."
W. C. Fields

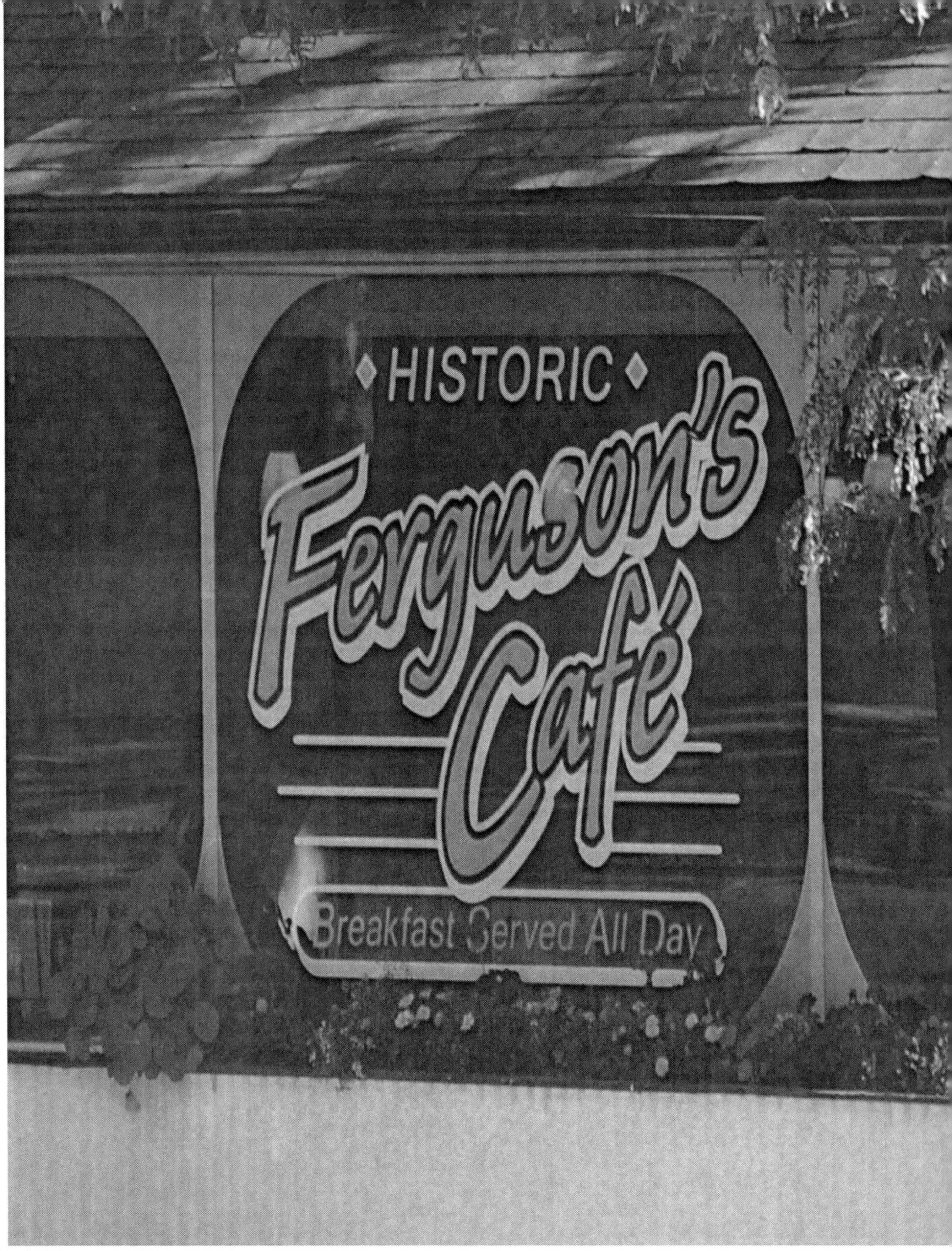
HISTORIC
Ferguson's
Café
Breakfast Served All Day

NAVY BEAN SOUP

Ferguson's Café, located in the historic Garland District, has great food and friendly service in a fun, relaxing atmosphere. Ferguson's features hearty breakfasts, delicious burgers and sandwiches, weekend dinner specials, and a full soda fountain menu. Locals cherish this neighborhood gem and many people feel they have stepped back in time when they walk through the door. It is decorated in classic 1950's-style, which no doubt is the reason several movies have been filmed at Ferguson's Café, perhaps most notably Benny and Joon starring Johnny Depp and Mary Stuart Masterson.

4 C. dried navy beans	**1.** Soak beans overnight in 1 gal. of water.
2 Tbsp butter	**2.** In a large stock pot, melt the butter and add the celery, onions, and carrots and cook until softened, about 5 minutes.
1 C. celery, diced	
1½ C. onions, diced	**3.** Add the beans with their water, the thyme, white pepper, bay leaf, and ham to the pot and bring to a boil over high heat.
2 C. carrots, diced	
1 tsp dried thyme	**4.** Simmer the soup on medium heat until the beans are soft, about 35–45 minutes, adding more water as necessary. Season to taste with salt and pepper.
1 tsp white pepper	
1 bay leaf	
2 C. cubed ham or one ham hock	
salt and pepper, to taste	

On September 25, 2011, Ferguson's Cafe suffered a fire that has crippled the business. A Fire Reconstruction Account has been established by the Garland Business District. Please feel to contact the Garland Business District to make a donation.

FERGUSON'S CAFÉ
804 WEST GARLAND AVENUE

"Me, sexy? I'm just plain ol' beans and rice."
Pam Grier

FERRANTE'S CLASSICO DEEP DISH PIZZA

Signature Tastes of SPOKANE

Ferrante's Marketplace Café has been serving fresh, traditional Italian family recipes with a creative approach since 2004. Ferrante's also features a busy marketplace with local jewelry, gifts, wine, and accessories. We offer a full lunch and dinner menu, family-style take out, catering, and we have eighteen flavors of gelato. Our knowledgeable and friendly staff make Ferrante's a Spokane original.

Dough:
4 C. warm water
¼ C. dry yeast
¼ C. sugar
11 C. "00" or all-purpose flour
½ C. sugar
¾ C. olive oil
2 Tbsp salt

Pizza Topping:
1 (16-oz.) can crushed tomatoes
2 (16-oz.) cans whole pear tomatoes, drained
1 handful chopped fresh basil
1 handful chopped fresh Italian parsley
12 garlic cloves, thinly sliced
2 C. grated parmesan cheese
extra virgin olive oil
salt and pepper

Dough:
1. Mix water, yeast, and ¼ C. sugar together in a small bowl and let stand for 10 minutes.
2. In a large bowl, mix the flour, ½ C. sugar, olive oil, and salt, then add the yeast liquid and mix until dough forms into a ball. If dough is too sticky add a little more flour.
3. Knead dough using a mixer fitted with a dough hook attachment (about 7–8 minutes) or by hand (about 10 minutes) until dough is smooth and elastic.
4. Divide dough in half and roll out the dough and press into 2 (9x13-inch) well-oiled sheet pans. Cover with plastic wrap or a clean towel and let rise in a warm place for 2–4 hours.

Pizza Topping:
1. Preheat oven to 400°F.
2. Uncover the dough and make 8–10 indentations with your fingers in each piece and spread half the crushed tomatoes, whole pear tomatoes, basil, and parsley on each crust and then top with sliced garlic, parmesan cheese, drizzle with extra virgin olive oil, and a pinch of salt and pepper.
3. Bake pizzas for 12–15 minutes or until edges and bottom are golden brown.

FERRANTE'S MARKETPLACE CAFÉ
4516 SOUTH REGAL AVENUE

"This recipe has been in our family for four generations. This is how my grandmother and her grandmother made pizza and it was at all our family gatherings."
Tony Ferrante, Owner

PERSIAN CELEBRATION RICE

Signature Tastes of SPOKANE

Fery's has been Spokane's premier caterer for over twenty years and we are ready to help with all of your party needs. Fery's has been serving some of the best food for private parties, weddings, office parties, fundraisers, and corporate events and we want to help make your next event a great success! Our staff will create artfully decorated platters, beautiful buffets, and elegant sit-down meals for any occasion including breakfasts, brunches, luncheons, dinners, cocktail and hors d'oeuvres parties, as well as outdoor picnics and barbeques. We are open Monday through Friday 9 am–6 pm, and Saturdays by appointment.

2 oranges
1 Tbsp canola oil
4 Tbsp onions, finely diced
1 lb. carrots, shredded
pinch of salt and pepper
2 Tbsp fresh lemon juice
½ C. chicken broth (or water)
½ C. dried barberries (found in specialty stores)
1 tsp ground saffron

Rice:
6 C. water
⅛ C. salt
2 C. white basmati rice
4 Tbsp canola oil
5 Tbsp water

Garnish:
½ C. blanched, slivered almonds

1. Remove the zest from one of the oranges, set zest aside. Peel the second orange, thinly slice the peels, then blanch peels twice in boiling water for 1–2 minutes to remove bitterness, set peels aside. Squeeze the juice from both oranges, set aside.

2. Heat 1 Tbsp of canola oil in a frying pan set over medium heat and sauté the onions, orange zest, blanched orange peels, and carrots. Season with a pinch of salt and pepper.

3. Once the onions are soft, add the orange juice, lemon juice, ½ C. chicken broth, barberries, and saffron, and bring to a boil. Reduce heat and simmer for 5 minutes. Set aside.

4. Meanwhile, bring 6 C. water to a boil in a medium sauce pan. Add ⅛ C. of salt and the basmati rice and boil for 10 minutes, making sure liquid does not boil over. Remove from heat, drain rice in a colander, and rinse the rice with water to remove excess salt.

5. In a large non-stick pot, add 4 Tbsp canola oil, 5 Tbsp water, ⅓ of the cooked rice, ½ of the carrot mixture (plus liquid). Layer another ⅓ of the rice, the remaining carrot mixture, and top with final ⅓ layer of rice (you can add 1–2 Tbsp of butter on top of the rice at this step if you prefer). Cover the pot with a lid and cook over medium heat for 10 minutes, or until steam appears. Remove the lid, and place a clean kitchen towel over the pot, then recover with the lid so that no steam can escape. Reduce heat to low and cook for another 45 minutes. Remove from heat and let rice rest for 5 minutes.

6. Remove the lid and the towel and gently scoop rice onto a serving platter and detach any crust on the bottom of the pan with a spatula, then break it into small pieces and arrange it on top of the rice. Garnish with blanched, slivered almonds.

FERY'S CATERING
421 SOUTH COWLEY STREET

"Let us help you with your party needs so that you can enjoy yourself without all the added stress of serving great food."
Fery Haghighi, Owner and Chef

BISCUITS WITH SAUSAGE GRAVY

The Flying Pig is located in the Spokane International District on East Sprague just minutes from downtown. We feature a menu of generously built cold and grilled sandwiches for both breakfast and lunch. The Flying Pig represents a dream come true for a mother-daughter team. We are having as much fun with the food as we are with the customers who come through our doors. Everyone is a "regular" at The Pig.

Sausage Gravy:
2 links of Italian sausage
¼ C. oil
½ C. flour
4½ C. of 2% milk
1¼ tsp black pepper
½ tsp salt

Biscuits:
2 C. all-purpose flour
1 Tbsp sugar
½ tsp baking soda
1 Tbsp baking powder
¼ tsp salt
5 Tbsp unsalted butter, cold, cut into pieces
½ C. buttermilk
½ C. heavy cream

Sausage Gravy:
1. Peel casings off of the Italian sausage and place in a food processor to finely chop.
2. Heat the oil in a sauce pan over medium heat, add sausage and cook until browned.
3. Add the flour to the pan, stir and cook for 1 to 2 minutes.
4. Gradually add the milk, whisking constantly.
5. Add the salt and pepper and cook on low heat for an additional 10–15 minutes until gravy is thick. If the gravy is too thick, add small amounts of additional milk.

Biscuits:
1. Preheat oven to 350°F.
2. Combine all the dry ingredients in a bowl.
3. Using a pastry blender, cut in the butter and blend until the mixture resembles coarse meal.
4. Gradually add the buttermilk and heavy cream until just combined.
5. On a lightly floured surface, roll out the biscuit dough to about 1-inch thickness. Cut out approximately 12 rounds with a biscuit cutter or a juice glass. Place biscuits onto a baking sheet close together, but not touching. Bake biscuits for about 15–20 minutes, until golden.
6. Serve the biscuits with the sausage gravy spooned over top.

THE FLYING PIG
1822 EAST SPRAGUE AVENUE

"Pig, you are cleared for take-off."
Erin Rauth and Marsha Loiacono, Owners

CLAM CHOWDER

Frankie Doodle's, located in the heart of downtown Spokane, has been a favorite restaurant among locals since 1981. You can hardly miss the sign from the freeway, and once you step inside this cozy and quirky old-fashioned coffee shop, you'll be met with warm smiles and great food.

Signature Tastes of SPOKANE

6 potatoes, peeled, diced

4 celery stalks, finely chopped

4 C. onions, finely chopped

2 carrots, finely chopped

1 (3-lb., 3-oz.) can of sea clams, drained, juice reserved

1 C. white wine

1 Tbsp granulated garlic

1 Tbsp white pepper

1 qt. hot water

2 C. powdered creamer

2 C. country gravy mix

4 Tbsp clam base

1. In a large pot, boil the potatoes, celery, onions, and carrots in 6 qt. of water.

2. In a separate pan, sauté the clams in the white wine until liquid evaporates.

3. When the potatoes in the large pot are soft, add the clams, garlic, and white pepper.

4. Mix 1 qt. of hot water with the powdered creamer and gravy mix and stir well. Stir into the soup and add the clam base and the reserved clam juice. Simmer the soup until thick and creamy.

FRANKIE DOODLE'S
30 EAST THIRD AVENUE

"We've been serving great food in Spokane since 1981!"
Linda Peterson and Kevin Miller, Co-owners

Our 100-year-old pancake recipe originally came from the mother of Pat Jepison. Mrs. Jepison learned it from her mother when she was a very young girl in 1921. Mrs. Jepison is ninety-five years old and is still alive today. We shop daily to find the largest and freshest eggs, super-extra thick bacon and use the best time-proven recipes. At each Frank's we crack 15,000 eggs and grill 2.5 tons of hash browns per month . . . all one breakfast at a time!

3 C. buttermilk powder
1 qt. pasteurized eggs
with citric acid
3 C. fine sugar
2 C. soybean oil
1 gal. enriched H&R
flour
1½ C. baking powder
1 Tbsp baking soda

1. Mix all ingredients together. Let mixture rise then whip again.

2. Pour batter onto heated griddle and flip when edges are dry.

"He who goes to bed hungry dreams of pancakes."
Proverb quotes

TRADITIONAL EGG SALAD

The Garland Sandwich Shoppe is located in the eclectic Garland Business District. "The Shoppe" is owned and operated by Kristen Speller, an Inland Northwest Culinary Academy graduate who takes great pride in supporting local businesses. The ingredients used in all sandwiches and salads are purchased from other local businesses. To ensure the highest quality and freshness, meats are sliced in-house daily, produce is purchased locally in small quantities, and all bread is bought daily from a local bakery. The Shoppe offers delicious Panini and deli-style sandwiches, housemade pasta salad, hand-tossed salads, and a variety of soups that are prepared in-house daily.

1 dozen hard-boiled eggs, peeled and cooled

1½ C. mayonnaise

¼ C. stone-ground mustard

¼ C. diced dill pickle

salt and pepper, to taste

1. Dice eggs and place in large chilled bowl.

2. Fold in remaining ingredients.

3. Season to taste with salt and pepper.

Note: You can substitute yellow mustard for the stone-ground mustard or sweet relish for the dill pickle. For an extra kick, try adding fresh, diced jalapeños or a dash of curry powder. The egg salad can be served on its own, on top of mixed greens, or between two slices of your favorite bread.

GARLAND SANDWICH SHOPPE
3903 NORTH MADISON STREET

"Remember, break the chain—support local businesses!"
Kristen Speller, Chef and Owner

GARLAND DRINKERY

COOL
NEW
BAR!
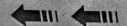

WHAT
WHISKY
WILL NOT
CURE,
THERE IS NO
CURE FOR

PINK LEMONADE

Local owners Bill and Deborah Weisgerber opened The Garland Avenue Drinkery in the historic Garland District in March 2011. This hip, cozy bar houses three flat-screen televisions, offers free wireless internet, a pinball machine, a jukebox, and an outdoor patio. With lots of drink specials, late-night food, and live music, the Garland Avenue Drinkery is a great addition to the neighborhood, redefining the district's nightlife scene.

1½ oz. vodka

splash of triple sec

2 oz. cranberry juice

½ lime

½ lemon

2 pinches of sugar

1. Fill a cocktail shaker with ice and add the vodka, triple sec, and cranberry juice. Squeeze the lime and lemon into the shaker and add 2 pinches of sugar. Shake well and serve on the rocks in a collins glass.

GARLAND AVENUE DRINKERY

828 WEST GARLAND AVENUE

"We just wanted to create a nice place for people to come to after work or a long day."
Deborah Weisgerber, Owner

71

ARTICHOKE PIE

The Garland Pub & Grill opened in March 2010 and is a fun neighborhood pub with great food and drinks. If you live in the neighborhood or come from afar, our friendly staff will always make you feel like a regular.

1 C. cubed mozzarella cheese

8 oz. artichoke hearts, drained and diced

½ C. diced pepperoni

¼ C. grated Monterey jack cheese

4 eggs, beaten

1 frozen pie shell

1. Preheat oven to 350°F.

2. Mix all the ingredients together in a bowl and pour into pie shell.

3. Bake for 45–50 minutes, or until the center of the pie is set. Cool and slice.

GARLAND PUB & GRILL
3911 NORTH MADISON STREET

"Live, Love, Laugh!"
motto of Garland Pub & Grill

AEGEAN CHICKEN

For over fourteen years The Globe Bar & Grille has been considered by those in the know as the hidden jewel of Spokane's downtown restaurant scene. With its unassuming charm, one normally doesn't expect to find the level of innovative cuisine served here. Quietly becoming a destination spot for guests from around the world, The Globe has built a reputation for hospitality and world class cuisine.

¼ C. olive oil

pinch of crushed
red pepper flakes

2 (7-oz.) chicken breasts,
halved, pounded, coated
with flour

1 Tbsp minced garlic

¾ C. Kalamata olives

¾ C. artichoke hearts

¾ C. diced tomatoes

2 C. white wine

3 Tbsp butter

½ C. feta cheese,
crumbled

small handful of
fresh spinach

2 C. cooked white rice

1. In a large skillet heat the olive oil and pepper flakes over medium-high heat. Add the chicken breasts and sauté for 4–5 minutes. When chicken is almost cooked through add the garlic, olives, artichoke hearts, and tomatoes and sauté for a few more minutes.

2. Deglaze pan wine and butter and cook until sauce is thickened.

3. Add the feta cheese and spinach and cook until spinach is wilted. Serve over white rice.

THE GLOBE BAR & GRILLE

204 NORTH DIVISION STREET

"Play with your food!"
Howard Bateman, Chef

ORANGE-GINGER DESSERT TOPPING

In China, family-style service allows all diners to share and experience many flavors, textures, and ingredients. We do the same. Gordy's food reflects the use of many kinds of spices, not just chile hotness. Ginger, garlic, and citrus plus the signature Sichuan peppercorn (Hua Jiao) are liberally used as well. Desserts are rare in Chinese cooking; traditionally, fresh fruit is a common meal ender, especially oranges, because their color is said to remind one of money. To satisfy the sweet tooth of Western diners we have taken some traditional Chinese ingredients and combined them into a topping especially fit for creamy desserts like ice cream, cheesecake, or crème brûlée. Enjoy!

8 Valencia oranges

2 C. sugar

2 C. water

1 Tbsp fresh ginger, grated

1 tsp dark soy sauce

½ tsp sambal olek paste (optional)

1. Peel the oranges and thinly slice the peels. Blanch the orange peels twice in a pot of boiling water for 1–2 minutes each time to remove the bitterness and reserve. Juice the oranges and reserve juice.

2. Combine sugar, water, ginger, soy sauce, and sambal olek in large sauce pan and simmer over medium-low heat, stirring occasionally, until liquid has reached a thin-syrup consistency. Do not boil over.

3. Add reserved orange peels and juice to the syrup and reduce to desired thickness, remove from heat. Allow to cool slightly and spoon over your favorite dessert.

GORDY'S SICHUAN CAFÉ
501 EAST THIRTIETH AVENUE

"Our small restaurant honors the traditions of China's cuisine with an emphasis on the rustic styles of the Sichuan province. We look forward to welcoming you to our little slice of culinary heaven!"
Jayme Crafts, Co-owner

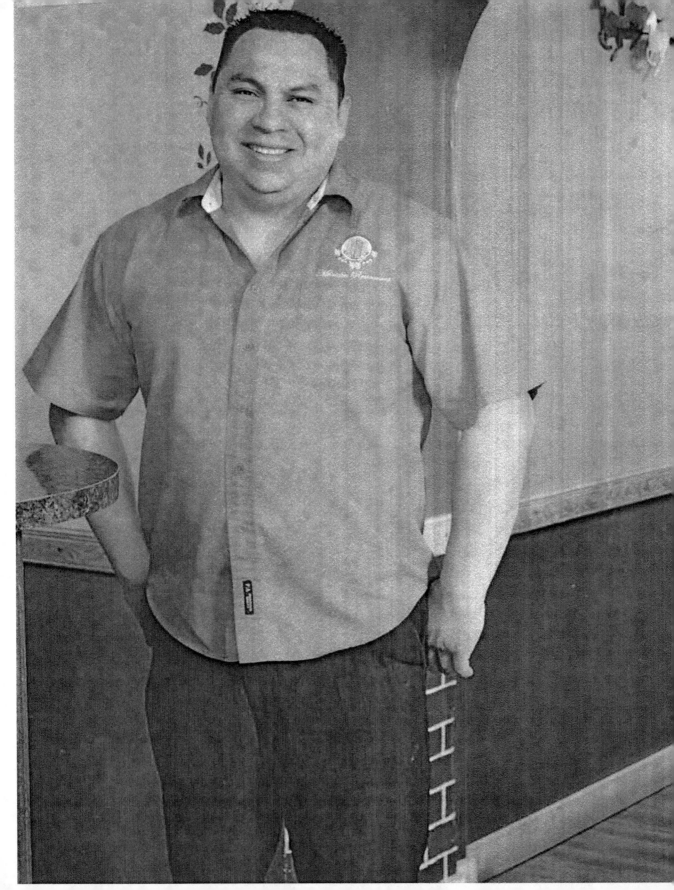

CHICKEN WITH MOLE SAUCE

At Hacienda Las Flores, owners Jorge and Adriana Hernandez provide warm hospitality, in a bright and festive interior — everything you'd expect from a family restaurant. Well known for their enormous portions, patrons certainly get their money's worth. Enjoy their signature tortilla chips served with refried beans with cheese, two kinds of salsa, and a mix of cabbage, onions, jalapeños, and cilantro. The menu offers plenty of traditional Mexican dishes so be sure to come hungry!

2 lb. boneless chicken breasts
5 C. of water
1 C. chopped celery
1 C. chopped onion
1 tomato, cut in half
½ tsp salt
½ C. canola oil
½ C. Dona Maria brown mole sauce
4 Tbsp peanut butter
1½ Tbsp ground cinnamon
2 Tbsp sugar
½ C. ketchup
1½ C. tomato juice
2 C. chicken broth

1. Place chicken breasts in a large pot and add the 5 C. of water, onion, celery, tomato, and ½ tsp of salt. Bring to a boil, reduce heat, cover, and simmer until chicken is cooked through, about 20–25 minutes. Remove chicken, cut into strips (fajita style), and set aside. Strain and reserve the chicken broth to make the mole.
2. Heat the canola oil in a large pot over medium heat. Add the mole sauce and stir to dissolve.
3. Next stir in the peanut butter and mix well.
4. Stir in the sugar and cinnamon.
5. Finally, add the ketchup, tomato juice, and chicken broth and stir well. Simmer the mole for 15 minutes, uncovered, stirring frequently.
6. Add the chicken strips to the mole sauce for a few minutes to reheat. Add more chicken broth if sauce is too thick.
7. Serve the chicken mole with Mexican rice, refried beans, or whole beans.

"We are excited to share our family recipes from Mexico City with you. Muy Bueno!"
Jorge and Adriana Hernandez, Owners

Spinach Salad with Strawberry Balsamic Dressing

Located in beautiful Liberty Lake, Washington, Hay J's Bistro is one of the Inland Empire's greatest hidden treasures. Since opening in 2006 it has provided a dining experience that has drawn a loyal following. The moment guests walk through the door, they are surrounded by the aromas of gourmet cuisine, a hospitable team of professionals, and a warm bistro ambiance. Our goal at Hay J's is to provide a dining experience that stimulates the senses and creates lasting memories. We invite you to join us for an outing of culinary delight and discover the jewel that we call Hay J's Bistro.

Dressing:
2½ C. fresh strawberries
2 tsp dried basil
2 tsp dried oregano
⅓ tsp dried thyme
1 tsp minced garlic
1½ tsp salt
1½ tsp pepper
⅓ tsp red pepper flakes
1¼ C. balsamic vinegar
2 tsp sugar
1¼ C. olive oil

Salad:
2-4 C. fresh spinach
1 C. sliced strawberries
¼ C. red onion, julienned
¼ C. toasted, slivered almonds

1. Place the strawberries in a food processor and puree.

2. Add the remaining ingredients except the olive oil and pulse a few times to mix well.

3. With the motor running, drizzle olive oil through the top in a small stream until oil is well combined.

4. Toss a small amount of dressing with a handful of fresh spinach, sliced strawberries, red onion, and almonds. Feel free to top the salad with a piece of your favorite white fish or scallops.

Hay J's Bistro
21706 East Mission Avenue

"Make your reservations today and discover an exquisite dining experience at Hay J's Bistro."
Patrick Fechser and Rhonda Entner, Co-owners

Spinach and Artichoke Egg Rolls

Herbal Essence Café's unique Northwest cuisine offers selections that will leave every customer satisfied and send them off telling everyone of the amazing experience they had. We are located a block and a half from the INB Performing Arts Center tucked inside a gorgeously restored brick building. Here you'll find a warm and inviting atmosphere mixed with excellent service to ensure an intimate evening or a quick lunch on the go. The staff at Herbal Essence is welcoming and knowledgeable and prepared to help you enjoy your dining experience to the fullest. Our extensive wine selection ensures the perfect selection to compliment every meal.

½ of 1 yellow onion, diced
½ C. shredded parmesan cheese
1 lb. frozen chopped spinach
1½ C. artichoke hearts, roughly chopped
1 C. of mayonnaise
1 Tbsp roasted garlic
1 tsp black pepper
1 package of egg roll wraps (6-inch)
butter or oil for frying

1. Combine the ingredients from the onion through the black pepper in a bowl and mix well.

2. Cut one square egg roll wrapper in half corner to corner to make two triangles. Scoop a little spinach artichoke filling into each wrapper and roll it up.

3. Heat a sauté pan over high heat, add the butter or oil and fry the egg rolls until golden brown on the outside. Serve with a sweet chili or sweet and sour dipping sauce.

Herbal Essence Café
115 North Washington Avenue

"It may be the way the cookie crumbles on Madison Avenue, but in Hong Kong it's the way the egg rolls."
Robert Orben, American humorist

BARBEQUE SAUCE

Signature Tastes of SPOKANE

3 Tbsp oil	**1.** In a large stock pot, heat the oil over medium heat and add the diced celery, onion, chili powder, and cayenne pepper. Stir occasionally until onion and celery are soft.
5 stalks of celery, small dice	
1 red onion, small dice	**2.** Add the cola and the ketchup and bring to a boil. Boil for 20 minutes or until sauce is thickened, stirring frequently.
1 Tbsp chili powder	
1 Tbsp cayenne pepper	**3.** Shut off the heat and stir in the brown sugar and liquid smoke. Let the sauce stand for 15 minutes, stirring at least twice during this time. The barbeque sauce tastes better the next day, stir well before serving.
1 qt. regular cola	
1 (114-oz.) container of ketchup	
1 lb. dark brown sugar	Note: Recipe makes about 1 gal. of barbeque sauce.
1 C. liquid smoke	

HEROES & LEGENDS
825 WEST RIVERSIDE AVENUE

Smoked Monterey Jack and Chicken in Phyllo

Hills' Restaurant & Lounge has been in business since 1993 and was originally named Hills' Someplace Else. We have been at our current location since 2007. We keep a vegetable and herb garden on our roof during the summer and were recently featured on the Food Network's Diners, Drive-ins, and Dives. We are just one block south of Riverfront Park and the INB Performing Arts Center. Open Tuesday through Saturday for lunch and dinner and Sunday for dinner only. We serve a unique blend of Asian, Southwestern, and European-influenced dishes using local ingredients.

1 lb. skinless, boneless chicken breast, diced
1 Tbsp Hills' firecracker spice blend (or Cajun seasoning mix*)
1 Tbsp chopped parsley
½ Tbsp chopped basil
½ C. dry white wine
1½ C. smoked Monterey jack cheese, grated
½ C. clarified butter
1 package phyllo dough sheets, thawed

*Cajun seasoning mix
1 tsp white pepper
1 tsp garlic powder
1 tsp onion powder
1 tsp cayenne pepper
1 tsp paprika
1 tsp black pepper

1. Heat ¼ C. of clarified butter in a large skillet over medium-high heat and sear chicken until cooked through.
2. Add the spice blend, parsley, and basil and stir.
3. Add the wine to deglaze the pan.
4. Add grated cheese and mix until the cheese is just melted.
5. Pour chicken filling mixture into a shallow sheet pan and refrigerate for a few hours until set.
6. Cut chicken filling mixture into 8 triangles.
7. Preheat oven to 350°F. Brush one phyllo sheet with clarified butter and fold into thirds. Place one triangle of the chicken filling onto phyllo sheet and fold over the phyllo to form a tight triangular package, being sure to not leave the corners open, and place on a sheet pan. Repeat process with remaining phyllo and chicken filling to make 8 packages.
8. Brush tops with more clarified butter and bake for 15 minutes, or until golden brown.

Hills' Restaurant & Lounge
401 West Main Avenue

"We like to have fun, our employees are sincere, our food is unpretentious, and we honestly feel our customers are part of our family."
Dave Hill, Chef and Co-owner of Hill's with brother Steve and mother Betty

WHITE CHEDDAR CRAB BISQUE

The 9th Street Bistro is located inside Huckleberry's Natural Market, which has been Spokane's leading natural and organic food provider for over fourteen years. The 9th Street Bistro provides classic and alternative dining for those seeking a natural, earth-friendly approach to cooking and living. The Bistro serves breakfast, lunch, and dinner with a rotating seasonal menu and strives to use local and fresh ingredients to support the local farms and producers in the Northwest.

1 C. unsalted butter 1 medium white onion, diced	**1.** Melt the butter in a 6 qt. pot over medium heat and add the onion and garlic and sauté until soft and golden.
3 Tbsp minced garlic 1 pt. pale ale-style beer	**2.** Add the pale ale and bring to a simmer, then reduce liquid by half, approximately 12 minutes.
12 C. heavy cream	**3.** Add the heavy cream and bring to a boil, stirring constantly so liquid does not boil over.
1 lb. Dungeness crab meat, broken into small pieces	**4.** Add the crab meat, reduce the heat, and simmer until liquid is reduced by ¼, approximately 15 minutes, or until thick.
8 oz. aged sharp white cheddar cheese, grated (such as Cougar Gold) salt and pepper, to taste	**5.** Turn off the heat and slowly add the grated cheddar, stirring constantly so that the cheese doesn't stick. Keep stirring in the cheese until it has completely melted and bisque has thickened. Season to taste with salt and pepper.

HUCKLEBERRY'S 9TH STREET BISTRO
926 SOUTH MONROE STREET

"It has been my pleasure to be a part of such a great community cornerstone that is Huckleberry's. I will continue to provide fresh, local fare to the people of Spokane and the surrounding area, as well as push the boundaries for organic, vegetarian, vegan, and gluten-free food choices."
Nicholas Marinovich, Executive Chef and Manager

JAMAICAN JERK BURRITO

Ionic Burritos is hands down a Spokane favorite, winning The Inlander Reader's Poll for "Best Burrito" ten years in a row. Using only the freshest ingredients is one reason Ionic makes the best burritos in town — plus all the sauces and salsas are made in-house. Ionic offers a great range of menu items from the traditional burrito to the more unique, like our Jamaican Jerk Burrito. Ionic also offers plenty of vegetarian and vegan options and our outstanding customer service will keep you coming back.

Jamaican Jerk Sauce:
10 jalapeños
14 garlic cloves
3 bunches green onions, ends trimmed
½ C. ground allspice
1 C. brown sugar
4 Tbsp dried thyme leaves
2 tsp cinnamon
1 tsp nutmeg
¼ C. soy sauce
¼ C. barbeque sauce

Jamaican Jerk Burrito:
tomato basil tortilla
cooked rice
black beans
grilled chicken, cubed
shredded Monterey jack cheese
sliced cabbage
diced cucumbers
shredded carrots
chopped cilantro
Jamaican jerk sauce
crushed pineapple

Jamaican Jerk Sauce:
1. Place the jalapeños, garlic, and green onions in a blender and blend into a paste.
2. Mix the allspice, brown sugar, thyme, cinnamon, and nutmeg together in a small bowl and stir into the paste.
3. Mix the soy sauce and barbeque sauce together, add to paste, and mix well.

Jamaican Jerk Burrito:
1. Add any or all of the ingredients to the tomato basil tortilla, top with Jamaican jerk sauce and crushed pineapple, fold up the burrito, enjoy!

IONIC BURRITOS
1415 NORTH HAMILTON STREET

"I was eating burritos with this girl and she asked me to be her prom date. How could I say no? We went and had a great time."
Josh Hartnett

PINK TOPAZ MARTINI

Irv's is Spokane's hottest new bar. The 6000 square foot facility features two full bars, Irv's and Irv's Other Room. Happy hours are seven days a week with DJ's, dancing, karaoke and a whole host of specialty promotions. Our game room has three pool tables, four pinball machines, and so much more...!

sugar for rimming the glass

2–3 lemon slices

4 oz. Johnny Love Aloha pineapple flavored vodka

1 oz. Cointreau

splash of cranberry juice

twist of lemon

1. Place the sugar on a plate and rub a lemon wedge around the edge of a martini glass and twist the rim of the glass in the sugar to coat the rim.

2. Fill a cocktail shaker with ice and muddle the lemon slices in the bottom of the cocktail shaker. Add the vodka, Cointreau, splash of cranberry juice, and shake well. Strain into the sugar-rimmed glass and serve with a twist of lemon.

IRV'S

415 WEST SPRAGUE AVENUE

"Wanna know more about Irv's...? Come on in and see for yourself!"

LINGUINI WITH PRAWNS

Signature Tastes of SPOKANE

3 oz. extra virgin olive oil
6 jumbo prawns
3 oz. artichoke hearts, roughly chopped
1½ oz. mushrooms, sliced
1 Tbsp capers
1 Tbsp garlic, minced
1 Tbsp shallots, minced
5 oz. white wine
¼ C. lemon juice
pinch of salt and pepper
pinch of dried Italian herbs
3 oz. tomatoes, diced
2 Tbsp unsalted butter
12 oz. cooked linguini

Garnish:
pinch of fresh chopped parsley
pinch of fresh chopped basil
2 lemon wedges

1. In a large sauté pan, heat the oil over medium-high heat. Add the prawns, artichokes, mushrooms, capers, garlic, and shallots and sauté, stirring frequently, until shallots and garlic are soft.

2. Deglaze the pan with wine and lemon juice and quickly reduce the liquid by half, or until sauce becomes thick. Add a pinch of salt and pepper, pinch of dried herbs, the tomatoes, and butter, and sauté just until the butter is melted.

3. Add the cooked linguini to the pan, tossing frequently until pasta is hot. Divide pasta among two bowls, add three prawns to each plate. Garnish with fresh chopped parsley and basil, and a wedge of lemon.

ITALIAN KITCHEN
113 NORTH BERNARD STREET

"Support all local restaurants! We truly rely on every penny and we care passionately about our guest's experience."
Bryce Kerr, Owner

BLT Soup

Jack & Dan's began as a "Spirits Emporium" during prohibition in 1932 called Louie's Snappie Service! Anyone who could afford a phone call and was within a two-mile radius could get a "bucket of suds" delivered via motorcycle to their home. Later the business became known as Joey's until 1975. Jack Stockton and Dan Crowley III ran Joey's for roughly fourteen years before they finally changed the name forever (at least 'til now) to Jack & Dan's. Today, Jeffrey Donald Condill and Kevin MacDonald are full partners. Located near the Gonzaga University campus, Jack & Dan's is popular among students, sports fans, and anyone looking for great food and drink in a friendly atmosphere.

8 slices of bacon, finely diced
½ C. diced green onions
2 Tbsp butter
3 C. finely sliced iceberg lettuce
1 C. diced fresh tomatoes
½ C. flour
3½ C. chicken broth, heated to a simmer
1/8 tsp ground white pepper
1 C. heavy cream
¼ C. of mayonnaise
¼ C. of sour cream

1. In a 3-qt. pot, cook the bacon over medium-high heat until lightly browned (remove 3 Tbsp of bacon bits for garnish).

2. Add the butter and green onions to the bacon in the pot stir until onions are soft.

3. Stir in the lettuce and tomatoes and cook for about 2 minutes.

4. Add the flour and stir until blended.

5. Add the hot chicken broth and ground white pepper and stir. Heat soup to boiling, stirring constantly, then reduce the heat and simmer gently for about 5 minutes.

6. Add the heavy cream, stir, bring to a simmer, then remove from heat.

7. Mix together the sour cream and mayonnaise and serve each portion of soup with a dollop of the mixture, and top with the reserved bacon bits.

JACK & DAN'S
1226 NORTH HAMILTON STREET

Jack & Dan's is "Where Good Friends Meet!"
motto of Jack & Dan's

Established in 1986, Just American Desserts is a specialty bakery producing gourmet cakes, cheesecakes, and holiday desserts. Our desserts are unique in that we only use the finest, freshest ingredients showcasing traditional techniques and making desserts like no other in the region. We use no mixes or artificial ingredients to cut corners. Just American Desserts has stayed true to its mission – bringing quality products to our community for over twenty-five years!

1 (9-inch) pie shell, unbaked
2 eggs, at room temperature
1 C. granulated sugar
1 tsp vanilla extract
2 Tbsp Bourbon
½ C. all-purpose flour
½ C. unsalted butter, melted and cooled
1 C. chopped pecans
1 C. semisweet chocolate chips

1. Preheat the oven to 350°F.

2. In a large bowl, beat the eggs, then add the sugar, vanilla, and Bourbon and stir well.

3. Add the flour and butter and mix gently.

4. Fold in the pecans and chocolate chips.

5. Pour batter into a 9-inch unbaked pie shell.

6. Bake at 350°F for 35–40 minutes. Cool.

7. Serve with vanilla ice cream or sweetened whipped cream.

JUST AMERICAN DESSERTS
MULTIPLE LOCATIONS

"Celebrating with a Just American Desserts product becomes a family tradition. There is nothing more rewarding than making a bride's wedding cake and having her tell you that you also made her first birthday cake!"
Eva Roberts, Owner

J-WALK
BAKERY & BISTRO

Signature Tastes of SPOKANE

At the J-Walk Bakery & Bistro we pride ourselves on making our baked goods in small batches from scratch just like you would at home. We specialize in producing a variety of fresh baked cookies, scones, cupcakes, bars, toasted Paninis, salads, and amazing drinks. Our selection varies daily and we are happy to customize any order to your liking. We are located a half block east of Monroe Street near the Spokane Courthouse and YMCA. Grab a seat and spend some time with us or take something to go. We look forward to serving you!

⅔ C. unsalted butter
1½ C. granulated sugar
3 eggs
1 C. unsweetened cocoa powder
¾ tsp salt
¾ tsp baking powder
1 tsp instant espresso powder (optional)
2 tsp vanilla extract
1 C. all-purpose flour
1 C. semisweet chocolate chips

1. Preheat oven to 350°F and grease a 9x9-inch brownie pan.
2. In a microwave-safe bowl or in a sauce pan set on low heat, melt the butter, then add the sugar and stir until sugar is dissolved (mixture should be shiny on top but not bubbling).
3. Add the eggs, cocoa, salt, baking powder, espresso powder, and vanilla and stir until batter is smooth.
4. Add the flour and stir until just incorporated.
5. Stir in the chocolate chips.
6. Pour the batter into the prepared pan and smooth batter evenly with a spatula.
7. Bake the brownies approximately 30 minutes or until a knife inserted into the center of the pan comes out clean with moist crumbs (there should be no raw batter). Remove from the oven and let cool in the pan. Cut into squares and serve.

J-WALK BAKERY & BISTRO

917 WEST BROADWAY AVENUE

"Being a great baker doesn't require much skill or training, trust us! What it takes is a sense of humor and adventure!"
Morgana Walker, Owner and Operator

Signature Tastes of SPOKANE

Since 2003, owners Charlie and Teri Baziotis have been committed to making an affordable breakfast that is more than tasty with great service in a wonderful family atmosphere. Hours of business are Monday through Saturday 6 am to 8 pm and on Sundays 6 am to 2 pm. Come on up and try the best kept secret in Spokane – it's where old friends visit and new friends meet.

vegetable oil for frying
3 corn tortillas
2 tsp unsalted butter
3 oz. of ham, diced
¼ C. green or red peppers, diced
¼ C. onions, diced
3 eggs, lightly beaten
¼ C. tomatoes, diced
¼ C. cheddar cheese, grated
salt and pepper
½ C. avocado, diced
sour cream
salsa

1. In a pan or deep fryer, preheat oil to 350°F. Set out a plate lined with paper towels. Fry tortillas for 20–30 seconds per side until light golden but still soft and flexible (cook longer for more crispy shells). Remove from oil and gently bend tortillas to form taco shells and set aside to drain on paper towels.

2. In a skillet, melt the butter over medium heat until foam subsides. Add ham, peppers, and onions, and cook for 2–3 minutes, stirring frequently.

3. Pour in the eggs, turn heat to low, and cook, stirring occasionally until the eggs are set, about 1–2 minutes.

4. Add tomatoes and cheese, season to taste with salt and pepper, and cover with a lid until cheese is melted, about 1–2 minutes.

5. Spoon eggs into taco shells and top with avocado, sour cream, and salsa.

KALICO KITCHEN
2931 NORTH DIVISION STREET

"Stop in and become part of the Kalico's family – you'll love it."
Charlie and Teri Baziotis, Owners

103

Hearty Lentil and Italian Sausage Soup

Back in 1949, there were no plastic bags of shredded potatoes, no bags of mixed salad greens, no boxed pies, no boxed pancake mixes, no frozen pre-formed hamburger patties. And there were certainly no large plastic bags of Lentil and Italian Sausage Soup. Then, like now, if you wanted a particular item to serve in your home or your restaurant, you were obligated to make it from scratch. And so it goes, our soups and sauces, pies and potatoes, are always made from scratch because in 1949 there was no other way. It's really about pride and integrity in the products we serve. So take a trip back in time where more than sixty years after we opened, we still make your meal just like Grandma's kitchen — all from scratch! Remember, at Knight's Diner it is still 1949!

4 C. dry lentils
1 (46-oz.) can of chicken stock
1 (30-oz.) can of crushed tomatoes with liquid
1 lb. Sonnenburg's New York Style Italian sausage, cut into ½-inch slices
1 medium onion, diced
2 garlic cloves, sliced
2 stalks of celery, thinly sliced, diagonally
2 carrots, thinly sliced, diagonally
2 dried bay leaves
1 Tbsp "No Salt" seasoning
1 Tbsp parsley, dried or fresh chopped
2 oz. olive oil, divided
1 Tbsp butter

1. Place the lentils in an 8-qt. stock pot, add just enough water to cover the lentils. Add the chicken stock and tomatoes with their liquid and bring to a boil, then lower the heat to a slow boil and reduce (approximately 30–45 minutes).
2. Meanwhile, in a separate pan, heat 1 oz. of oil over medium heat and brown the sausage. Remove from the pan and drain on paper towels and then add to the soup.
3. In the same pan, add the remaining oil and butter and lightly sauté the onion, garlic, celery, and carrots over medium heat, approximately 5–7 minutes.
4. After lentils have reduced (30–45 minutes) add the sautéed vegetables, bay leaves, "No Salt" seasoning, and the parsley.
5. Simmer the soup until lentils are tender.
6. Transfer to crock pot set on low to hold or cool in shallow pans.
7. Serve with a sprig of fresh parsley and/or a dollop of sour cream.

Knight's Diner
2909 North Market Street

"The very best revenge...is living well."
Deral Green, Owner

Monday Specials
$-50

latte Special
Caramel $1.60

Egg Salad, mayo, and lettuce
served w/chips or pickle

Soups

? w/wild rice
Chowder

Broccoli w/Cheese
Roasted Red Pepper

SWEET AND SOUR DRESSING

Kowalski's Deli has been in business for over forty-nine years. It has always been a family owned and operated business. We have regulars who come in at least once a week – and sometimes more. We are located a few miles north of downtown Spokane on Division Street and we have an eat-in dining area, plenty of parking, and we also deliver within a five-mile radius. Come on up and see us or give us a call and we'll bring you lunch!

3 C. of sugar

1 C. of oil

1 C. of vinegar

1 ⅓ C. of ketchup

3 Tbsp Worchester sauce

1. Combine all the ingredients in a bowl and whisk to combine.

Note: At Kowalski's the sweet and sour dressing is served with a spinach salad topped with mushrooms, bacon, almonds, hard-boiled egg, and parmesan cheese.

KOWALSKI'S DELI
4407 NORTH DIVISION STREET

"My deli is my dream come true!"
Tyre Cooper, Owner

THE TRIPLE NON-FROWN BROWN COCONUT PORTER FLOAT

Signature Tastes of SPOKANE

The Lantern Tavern is an intimate space nestled right in the middle of the South Perry District on Spokane's South Hill. Though it may seem small, The Lantern is big on community spirit and has become an anchor of the South Perry Street neighborhood. Whether you are outside on the patio or tucked away inside, The Lantern is a great place to meet friends and enjoy a drink before or after dinner or after a stop at the Perry Street farmers' market.

1 can of Maui coconut porter

1½ scoops vanilla or coffee ice cream

whipped cream

chocolate syrup

1. Pour the Maui coconut porter into a 16 oz. pint glass or Belgium goblet. Let stand until the creamy head falls, then carefully add the ice cream (do not agitate) and let it stand for 3–5 minutes until the beer and melting ice cream form three brown layers. If done properly it will have a layered "Neapolitan" effect.

2. Garnish with whipped cream and drizzle chocolate syrup over the top (optional). Serve and enjoy!

THE LANTERN TAVERN

1004 SOUTH PERRY STREET

"There is sweet water inside a tender coconut. Who poured the water inside the coconut? Was it the work of any man? No. Only the Divine can do such a thing."
Early Hawaiian Settler

BUCKET OF LOVE

Latah Bistro is a small neighborhood restaurant that has been serving thoughtfully sourced casual fare since 2004. Chef David Blaine has worked closely with area farmers and the Bistro's customers to create a unique venue for showcasing food and wine that reflects the lifestyle and values of the region.

3.5 oz. unsalted butter, cold, cut into small pieces*

3.5 oz. bittersweet chocolate, finely chopped (no more than 60% cacao)

4 oz. granulated sugar

3 large eggs

½ tsp ancho chili powder

2 tsp ground cinnamon

*For the most accurate results, use a food scale to measure out first three ingredients.

1. Preheat oven to 350°F. For best results use a silicone mini muffin pan. If using metal pans, be sure to butter the tins so that the cakes do not stick.

2. Melt the chocolate and butter slowly in a double boiler, stirring constantly until chocolate is melted and smooth. Remove from heat.

3. Add the sugar and stir with a wire whisk until sugar is dissolved.

4. Add the eggs one at a time, whisking gently until eggs are incorporated.

5. Stir in the chili powder and cinnamon.

6. Divide batter among mini-muffin tins, filling each one two-thirds full. Bake until cakes are cooked through but still moist, about 20–23 minutes. Cool completely before removing from the pan.

Note: At the Bistro, the cakes are served in a parchment cone with powdered sugar sprinkled over the top.

LATAH BISTRO

4241 SOUTH CHENEY SPOKANE ROAD

"Relationships are what this restaurant is all about. From the farmer to the customer to the employee—it's the people that make this such a great place."
David Blaine, Chef

LeftBank

WINE BAR

Signature Tastes of SPOKANE

Over sixty wines by the glass are offered at Left Bank Wine Bar, which is located on the ground floor of the historic American Legion Building on Washington Street in downtown Spokane. Inspired by Venice's Caffe Florian, Left Bank Wine Bar has an atmosphere that aims to capture an elegant, European-style approach to one of the world's oldest and most popular beverages. Relax with a glass of wine and a cheese plate in the afternoon, champagne and dessert in the evening, or come in and enjoy live music every weekend.

Baked Brie:
balsamic reduction
(recipe follows)
brie cheese, at room
temperature (any size)
brown sugar
sliced, roasted almonds
dried cherries or
dried cranberries
2 sheets of phyllo dough
butter, melted
sliced apples or pears

Balsamic Reduction:
1½ C. balsamic vinegar
¼ –½ C. of brown
sugar (to taste)

Balsamic Reduction:
1. In a small sauce pan, bring balsamic vinegar to a boil, turn down the heat and simmer until reduced by half. Stir in brown sugar and simmer until it reaches syrup consistency and sticks to the back of a spoon. As it cools it will thicken.

Baked Brie:
1. Preheat oven to 450°F.
2. Cut the brie in half horizontally to form two equal layers, set aside the top layer.
3. Generously sprinkle the bottom layer of brie with brown sugar, coating the entire surface, then top with dried fruit and then the roasted almonds. Carefully place the top layer of brie over the dressed layer of brie to create a "sandwich." Wrap the brie in 2 sheets of phyllo dough and brush the outside layer with melted butter.
4. Place brie on a sheet pan and bake for 15 minutes or until phyllo is lightly browned and center of brie is soft and creamy.
5. Plate the baked brie and drizzle with balsamic reduction. Serve warm with fruit, such as thinly sliced apples or pears.

LEFT BANK WINE BAR
108 NORTH WASHINGTON STREET

"Our goal is to broaden the appeal of wine in a completely non-threatening way. We want our customers to sit back and relax and discover for themselves the beauty and depth of an Oregon pinot noir or the floral crispness of a viognier."
Aaron Kelly, Owner

PASTA WITH BACON, BLUE CHEESE, AND TOMATO

Signature Taste of **SPOKANE**

½ lb. radiatore pasta

½ C. extra virgin olive oil

3 garlic cloves, minced

¼ lb. bacon, cooked crisp and chopped

2 large heirloom tomatoes, chopped

½ C. blue cheese, crumbled

⅓ C. fresh basil, chopped

sea salt and black pepper, to taste

1. Add water to a large pot, season with a generous amount of sea salt, and bring to a boil. Add the pasta and cook to al dente firmness according to package directions, drain, but do not rinse. Pour pasta into a large bowl.

2. In a small skillet, heat the oil and garlic over medium heat until the garlic floats to the top of the oil. Remove from heat promptly.

3. Add the garlic-oil to the bowl with the pasta and toss well. Stir in the bacon, tomatoes, blue cheese, and basil. Season to taste with salt and pepper. Bon appétit!

LINDAMAN'S

1235 SOUTH GRAND BOULEVARD

"This has been a popular dish at the restaurant for twenty-five years!"
Merrilee Lindaman, Owner and Chef

Lion's Lair is a recently remodeled and expanded bar with an exciting atmosphere located in downtown Spokane. It's a great place to gather with friends and listen to live music or a DJ, or come in for games, pool, or enjoy our outdoor patio in warm weather – there is something for everyone here! Be sure to come and check out our unique pub food menu and specialty drinks.

¾ oz. Finlandia grapefruit vodka

¾ oz. Yazi ginger vodka

¾ oz. Hpnotiq liqueur

¾ oz. X-rated fusion liqueur

equal parts Red Bull and Monster Khaos

1. Fill a cocktail shaker with ice, add all of the ingredients and shake well. Serve straight up or on the rocks in a pint glass.

LION'S LAIR

205 WEST RIVERSIDE AVENUE

"A well-composed book is a magic carpet on which we are wafted to a world that we cannot enter in any other way."
Caroline Gordon

Luigi's Famous Smoked Salmon Lasagna

Signature Tastes of SPOKANE

Sauce:
½ C. unsalted butter
⅓ C. all-purpose flour
4 C. whole milk
1 tsp salt
½ tsp white pepper
¼ C. grated parmesan cheese
¼ C. grated Gruyère cheese
2 Tbsp dry sherry

Lasagna:
¼ C. grated cheddar
¾ C. grated mozzarella cheese
¾ C. grated provolone cheese
¾ C. grated parmesan cheese
1 lb. spinach lasagna noodles, cooked al dente
3 large tomatoes, peeled, seeded, and chopped
½ lb. mushrooms, thinly sliced
1¼ lb. smoked salmon, thinly sliced

Sauce:
1. In a sauce pan melt the butter over moderately-low heat. Add the flour to make a roux and cook for about 3 minutes, whisking constantly. Pour in the milk and bring to a boil, whisking constantly until mixture is thickened, about 10 minutes. Remove pan from heat and stir in the salt, white pepper, parmesan, Gruyère, and sherry. Set aside.

Lasagna:
1. Put a rack in middle of oven and preheat oven to 350°F.
2. Stir all of the cheeses together in a bowl.
3. Lightly oil a 9x13-inch baking dish and spread a thin layer of the sauce in the bottom. Follow with a layer of noodles, top with ⅓ of the sauce, half of the tomatoes, half of the mushrooms, half of the salmon, and ⅓ of the cheese mixture. Repeat process to make one more layer ending with the cheese mixture.
4. Top the lasagna with the remaining noodles and spread the remaining sauce over the noodles and top with remaining cheese mixture.
5. Bake the lasagna for 45 minutes to 1 hour, or until the top is golden.

Luigi's Italian Restaurant
245 West Main Avenue

"We hire the best people, buy the best-quality ingredients, and we do whatever it takes to make sure our customers are satisfied, full, and happy."
Marty Hogberg, Owner

At Luna we are committed to using locally-grown, seasonal, and sustainable ingredients, which helps us focus on building partnerships and creating a community. We proudly support local farmers and artisans of the Inland Northwest. We also know the importance of "going green" and presently we are the only restaurant in Spokane to compost and recycle all of our organic materials. Luna is a stand-alone restaurant in a neighborhood high atop Spokane's South Hill. There is plenty of parking and a sense of spacious freedom. Luna has a full service lounge, classic marble-top dining areas, and The Garden Room, a beautiful private dining room. There is a delightful rose-enclosed terrace and a magnificent flower garden courtyard for truly al fresco dining and lounging.

Coconut Custard:
1 C. half and half
1 C. heavy cream
1 C. coconut milk
1 tsp vanilla extract
1 egg
1 Tbsp flour
1 Tbsp corn starch
2 Tbsp granulated sugar
1 C. unsweetened coconut flakes

Coconut Cake:
1 C. unsalted butter, softened
1 lb. granulated sugar
1 tsp salt
4 eggs
1 lb. cake flour
2 tsp baking powder
1 tsp baking soda
1½ C. coconut milk
1 tsp vanilla extract

Butter Cream Frosting:
1 C. egg whites
2 C. confectioners' sugar
1 tsp vanilla extract
2 C. unsalted butter, softened

Garnish:
unsweetened toasted coconut

Coconut Custard:
1. In a small sauce pan, bring the half and half, heavy cream, coconut milk, and vanilla extract to a boil. Whisk together the egg, flour, corn starch, and sugar. Pour the egg mixture into the boiling cream and continue to cook, stirring constantly until the custard thickens to a pudding-like consistency. Immediately remove the custard from heat and stir in the coconut flakes. Transfer the custard to a plastic container and cover the entire surface area with plastic wrap and press into the custard to prevent a skin from forming, then refrigerate for at least 2 hours.

Coconut Cake:
1. Preheat oven to 325°F.
2. With a mixer, cream together the butter, sugar, and salt, then add the eggs one at a time, scraping down the sides of the bowl frequently. Stir together the flour, baking powder, and baking soda. Set the mixer to medium speed and add the flour-mixture a little at a time and mix until completely incorporated. Set the mixer to low speed and slowly add the coconut milk and vanilla extract.
3. Divide the batter among at least three greased, parchment-lined, 8-inch round cake pans and spread smooth with a spatula. Bake for 15–18 minutes or until a toothpick inserted in the center comes out clean. Cool completely and remove from pans.
4. To slice the cakes into layers, set cake on a flat, even surface, and cut each cake in half using a large serrated knife (you will need at least six layers). Set cake layers aside.

Butter Cream Frosting:
1. Using a mixer set on high speed, whip together the egg whites, sugar, and vanilla extract until stiff-peaks form, then slowly add small pieces of softened butter, whipping until frosting is smooth.

Cake Assembly:
1. Fill a piping bag fitted with a plain round tip with the butter cream frosting. Position one layer of cake on a turntable or cake stand and carefully pipe a ring of butter cream around the extreme edge of the cake, then fill in the ring with ⅕ of the cooled coconut custard. Set the next layer of cake on top of the first and repeat until there are five filled layers. The top layer is not filled with custard. Place the cake in the refrigerator for about 15 minutes to set.
2. Crumb-coat your cake by spreading a very thin layer of butter cream over the cake, then frost the whole cake with an even covering of ¼-inch of butter cream. Press toasted coconut into the sides and top of the cake and return to the refrigerator. Let chill for at least 1 hour before cutting.

FOCACCIA MEATLOAF

Signature Tastes of SPOKANE

1 loaf focaccia bread
1 C. milk
2 oz. olive oil
½ C. onions, small dice
3 lb. ground beef
4 eggs, lightly beaten
1 Tbsp kosher salt
1 tsp fresh ground black pepper
½ tsp ground ginger
½ C. ketchup
½ C. Heinz 57 sauce
½ C. red bell pepper, small dice

1. Preheat oven to 375°F.

2. Cut focaccia into small cubes and soak in the milk for 5 minutes.

3. In a small pan, sauté the onions in the olive oil over medium heat until onions are transparent.

4. In a large bowl, combine the ground beef, eggs, salt, pepper, ground ginger, ketchup, and Heinz 57 sauce and mix well.

5. Add the focaccia and milk mixture, onions, and peppers. Mix well and place into two loaf pans, pressing tightly. Hit the pans on the countertop a few times to eliminate air bubbles.

6. Bake meatloaf until internal temperature reaches 160°F, approximately 1 hour. Cool for 10 minutes before slicing.

THE LUXURY BOX
10512 EAST SPRAGUE AVENUE

CHICKEN POT PIE

Maggie's South Hill Grill opened in 2004 offering Spokane a unique and modern style of family dining. Located in the Lincoln Heights shopping area on the middle of Spokane's South Hill, this lovely bistro has revolutionized the way Spokane families dine out. Maggie's offers salads, sandwiches, pasta, grilled steaks and fish, as well as featured wines and beer. Entrée favorites include pan-seared ahi tuna, flat iron steak, and charbroiled barbeque chicken. Don't forget to try the chicken pot pie – a family favorite!

Signature Tastes of SPOKANE

8 qt. chicken stock, divided
2 Tbsp dried basil
2 Tbsp dried thyme
2 Tbsp dried sage
2 Tbsp dried oregano
3 bay leaves
½ C. butter or margarine
2 lb. carrots, small dice
2 lb. onion, small dice
2 lb. celery, small dice
2 Tbsp garlic, minced
4 lb. chicken, roasted, medium dice
3 lb. red potatoes, quartered, pre-roasted
2 C. margarine
1 lb. all-purpose flour
4 C. heavy cream
salt and pepper, to taste
4 C. frozen peas
4 C. frozen corn
pre-made, refrigerated pie crusts

1. Preheat oven to 500°F.
2. In a medium pot, add 2 qt. of the chicken stock, the dried basil, thyme, sage, oregano, and bay leaves and bring to a simmer to infuse the stock with the herbs.
3. In a very large stock pot, melt the ½ C. of butter or margarine over medium heat, then sauté the carrots, onions, celery, and garlic until onions are translucent. Add the diced chicken and potatoes and sauté for 5 minutes. Add the infused chicken stock plus the remaining 6 qt. of stock to the pot, and simmer for 20 minutes.
4. While the pot pie filling is simmering, melt the 2 C. of margarine in a large pan over medium heat and add the flour, whisking constantly to form a roux; cook, stirring frequently, for about 5 minutes. Set aside.
5. After the 20 minutes of simmering, add the heavy cream to the pot pie filling and bring back to a boil. Then add the roux and stir gently until filling thickens, about 5–10 minutes more. Remove from heat, add salt and pepper to taste, then stir in the frozen peas and corn.
6. Scoop chicken pot pie filling into oven-proof individual serving bowls. Cut the pre-made pie crusts to fit over the top of the bowl, cut several slits in the crust to allow steam to escape. Bake for 5–10 minutes or until crust is golden brown and filling is bubbling.

MAGGIE'S SOUTH HILL GRILL
2808 EAST TWENTY-NINTH AVENUE

"Our concept is casual, quick, and great food. We want everyone who comes here to feel comfortable, whether you're dressed for the symphony or you've just come from working on your house."
Maggie Boone, Owner

Curry Chicken Salad with Broccoli and Apricots

Main Market Co-op is a retail food co-op that is owned by its members. Membership is voluntary and anyone can become an owner – just $10 will get your started! We feature fresh local produce, local meat, eggs, dairy, regional wines, microbrews, artisanal cheeses, made-from-scratch deli selections (vegan and gluten free options available), locally roasted fair-trade coffees, body care and supplements, bulk flours, grains, and spices.

Signature Tastes of SPOKANE

Dressing:
½ C. golden balsamic vinegar
3 Tbsp Dijon mustard
2 Tbsp curry powder
½ C. extra virgin olive oil
¾ C. canola oil

Chicken Salad:
4 oz. boneless chicken breast, cooked and cubed
4 C. broccoli florets, lightly blanched and chilled
¼ C. toasted sliced almonds
¼ C. dried cranberries
¼ C. dried apricots, thinly sliced

1. In a blender or food processor, combine balsamic vinegar, Dijon mustard, and curry powder and process until smooth. With the motor running, add the oils in a slow steady stream until mixture is thick and creamy.

2. Add the chicken, broccoli, almonds, and dried fruits to a large mixing bowl then add about half the dressing (or to taste) to the chicken salad and mix well.

Main Market Co-op
44 West Main Avenue

"At Main Market Co-op we seek out high quality foods and merchandise from local, organic, and sustainable producers."
Jeanette Hamilton, General Manager

BELLUNO SCAMPI

Preparing and sharing great food is an expression of love and pride for Italians. Ginny and Jerry Amicarella want you to feel the amore as they share their southern Italian traditions with you.

10 oz. linguini
½ C. of reserved pasta water
¼ C. olive oil
1 Tbsp garlic, minced
6 jumbo shrimp
4 oz. tomatoes, chopped
salt and pepper, to taste
pinch of chopped fresh basil
pinch of chopped fresh parsley
Asiago cheese

1. Bring a large pot of salted water to a boil and cook the linguini to desired firmness. Reserve ½ C. of the pasta water before draining to make the sauce.

2. In a large sauté pan, heat the oil over medium-high heat and add the garlic, stir frequently until fragrant. Add the shrimp and tomatoes and cook for about 5 minutes over medium heat.

3. Add the cooked linguini to the pan and mix well. Add just enough of the reserved pasta water to create a sauce and toss until pasta is well coated and hot. Add salt and pepper to taste. Divide pasta and shrimp among two bowls and sprinkle with chopped basil and parsley. Serve with grated Asiago cheese, if desired.

MAMMA MIA'S
420 WEST FRANCIS AVENUE

"Made from scratch daily!"
Mamma Mia's slogan

HUCKLEBERRY SCONES

We are a small, family owned and operated restaurant in North Spokane that opened in 2007. Enjoy a cup of our locally roasted coffee or espresso with one of our fresh baked goods that we make from scratch using family recipes. Come in for lunch and have one of our sandwiches or Paninis or a fresh hand-tossed salad. During the summertime you can relax and enjoy your meal on our patio.

2 C. all-purpose flour,
plus more for dusting
⅓ C. granulated sugar
1 Tbsp baking powder
2 large eggs
⅔ C. heavy cream
½ C. of butter, cut into
cubes, softened
½ C. frozen huckleberries
1 egg for egg wash +
¼ C. water
granulated or turbinado
sugar for topping

1. Preheat oven to 400°F and line a baking sheet with parchment paper.

2. In a large bowl, stir together the flour, sugar, and baking powder.

3. Add the eggs, heavy cream, and butter and stir just until dough starts to hold together. Do not over mix.

4. Transfer dough to a well-floured surface and gently work in the huckleberries with your hands.

5. Shape the dough into an 8-inch circle and cut into 8 wedges and transfer scones to the parchment lined baking sheet.

6. Make the egg wash by whisking 1 egg with ¼ C. water then brush over scones and sprinkle with sugar.

7. Bake scones for 20–24 minutes or until tops are light brown.

MAPLE STREET BISTRO

5520 NORTH MAPLE STREET

"As a close-working family we love our customers and enjoy the ability to build relationships with them and our community!"
Deserae Cohrs, Owner

CARNAROLI SEARED SCALLOPS WITH LEMON ROASTED CAULIFLOWER SAUCE

Masselow's at Northern Quest Resort and Casino has the prestige of being the only AAA Four Diamond restaurant in Eastern Washington. Chef Bob Rogers and his team have created menus that feature Northwest inspired dishes and exceptional regional wines. Entrée selections change by the season to ensure the ingredients are at their peak. Our menu leans towards the simplistic, allowing the natural beauty, flavor, and quality to shine through. Masselow's is both elegant and comfortable with historical representations of the Kalispel tribe adorning the dining room walls.

Lemon Roasted Cauliflower Sauce:
1 head cauliflower, outside leaves removed
¼ C. extra virgin olive oil
2 Tbsp fresh lemon juice
2½ C. heavy cream (heated)
2 tsp fresh lemon juice
salt and pepper, to taste

Scallion Oil:
½ C. olive oil
¼ C. sliced scallions

Carnaroli Seared Scallops:
1/4 C. Carnaroli rice (or substitute Arborio)
12 extra large sweet scallops
2 Tbsp clarified butter
salt and pepper, to taste
1–2 Tbsp scallion oil
fresh celery leaves

Lemon Roasted Cauliflower Sauce:
1. Preheat oven to 350°F.
2. Mix the olive oil and 2 Tbsp of lemon juice together and rub the cauliflower generously with mixture. Pour any remaining liquid into the bottom of a roasting pan and add a small amount of water (½-inch). Place cauliflower on a rack in the roasting pan and cover pan tightly with foil. Roast until cauliflower is fully cooked and tender, approximately 1½ hours.
3. Allow cauliflower to cool slightly then break it apart and place into a blender or food processor. With the motor running, slowly add the heated heavy cream and 2 tsp of lemon juice until the sauce is a very thick but smooth puree. Season to taste with salt and pepper.

Scallion Oil:
1. Place oil and scallions in a food processor and blend together.

Carnaroli Seared Scallops:
1. Place the rice in a food processor and grind the rice until it is a fine powder.
2. Dust the scallops with the rice powder.
3. In a pan, heat the clarified butter over medium-high heat and sear the scallops until a very light, crispy surface forms, turning once.
4. Serve scallops with lemon roasted cauliflower sauce and a few drops of scallion oil. Garnish with fresh celery leaves.

MASSELOW'S
100 NORTH HAYFORD ROAD

"Every day I come to work I enjoy watching my team grow while at the same time learning so much from all of them."
Bob Rogers, Chef

PEANUT BUTTER PIE

At MAX, you'll find eclectic cuisine and an award-winning menu featuring more than 100 items. Our extensive wine list boasts more than 500 labels and every Wednesday you can enjoy half-price bottles of wine. We offer late-night dining with a full menu until close, two happy hours daily from 3–6 pm and again from 9 pm to close, and we feature an à la carte brunch menu on Saturday and Sunday. Max's lounge menu features more than seventy-five of the most innovative cocktails and martinis from retro to nouveau, and live music fills the room from 9 pm–1 am Friday and Saturday nights.

Peanut Butter Brittle Base:
2 tsp vinegar (cider or white)
¾ C. light corn syrup
¾ C. honey
¼ C. water
1½ C. granulated sugar
1 C. salted butter
5¼ C. smooth peanut butter
1 tsp vanilla extract
1½ tsp baking soda

Chocolate-Truffle Top:
2 lb. semisweet or dark chocolate, finely chopped
4 C. heavy cream, divided
1½ C. salted butter

Peanut Butter Brittle Base:
1. Grease a 10-inch springform pan and set aside.
2. In a medium pot, add the vinegar and swirl around, coating the sides and bottom of the pot, and dump out excess. Do not let the pot dry since the acid will prevent the sugar from crystallizing.
3. Add the corn syrup, honey, water, and sugar in order and mix with a clean, dry spoon. Place a candy thermometer on the side of the pot and bring mixture to boil over medium heat until temperature reaches 290°F, then turn heat to medium-low
4. Add the butter, peanut butter, and vanilla extract and whisk constantly until smooth.
5. Stir in the baking soda, which should foam up and make the mixture turn pale. Immediately pour the brittle base into a well-greased 10-inch springform pan. Spread evenly to create a flat bottom layer and refrigerate at least 20 minutes.

Chocolate Truffle Top:
1. In double boiler, add the chocolate, 2 C. of heavy cream, and butter and stir over medium heat until the chocolate and butter are melted and mixture is smooth, remove from heat.
2. Using a mixer, whip the remaining 2 C. of heavy cream until stiff peaks form. Fold into the melted chocolate mixture.
3. Pour chocolate on top of the peanut butter brittle layer of the springform pan. Chill for 10 hours. Cut into your desired number of pieces.

Signature Tastes of SPOKANE

MAX AT MIRABEAU
1100 NORTH SULLIVAN ROAD

"There's always something happening at the MAX. And . . . we are a five-time Epicurean Delight award-winner."
Andy Rooney, General Manager

135

Dining out is a memorable experience at Milford's. We've been serving fine fare in a warm, early-twentieth century setting since 1979. You will enjoy the freshest seafood and fish available in Spokane where chef/owner Jerry Young has been preparing beautiful dining experiences for nearly three decades. Using his creativity and the freshest fish, meat, poultry, and ingredients available, Jerry delivers magic on a plate to you and your dinner companions. When you want to treat yourself, a friend or loved one, or a business client, Milford's atmosphere and Jerry's culinary treats will always satisfy.

½ C. unsalted butter
3 C. diced peppers
3 C. diced onion
3 C. sliced mushrooms
2 C. green onion, chopped
1 stalk of celery, diced
2¼ C. Johannesburg riesling
3 C. heavy cream
1 Tbsp lobster base
1 Tbsp chicken base
½ oz. black pepper
1 oz. granulated garlic
1 oz. basil
1 oz. celery salt
1 tsp cayenne pepper
1 lb. crawfish tail meat
½ lb. shrimp meat
puff pastry, thawed
1 egg, beaten, mixed with
¼ C. water

Roux:
½ C. unsalted butter
⅓ C. all-purpose flour

1. Preheat oven to 400°F.

2. In a large pan, melt the butter over medium heat and sauté the vegetables until tender.

3. Add riesling and cook over medium heat about 10 minutes, stirring occasionally.

4. Meanwhile, in separate pan make the roux by melting ½ C. butter over medium heat. Whisk in the flour and stir constantly until a thick, smooth paste forms. Cook roux for 3–4 minutes, remove from heat, and set aside.

5. Add the heavy cream, bases, seasonings, crawfish, and shrimp to the vegetable mixture and let simmer another 5 minutes. Check seasonings and stir in the roux until thick. Let cool slightly before putting in oven-proof bowls. Cover bowls with puff pastry and brush with egg wash and bake until pastry is golden brown, about 8–10 minutes.

MILFORD'S FISH HOUSE
719 NORTH MONROE STREET

"That's kinda like my old man told me one time, Lynn. The only thing better than a crawfish dinner, is five crawfish dinners."
*Coach Red Beaulieu: **The Waterboy***

Vegan Meatloaf

Considered one of Spokane's finest restaurants, Mizuna offers a dynamic seasonal menu featuring the best fresh, local, organic Northwest ingredients. We are situated in the heart of downtown, housed in a charming turn-of-the-century building with tall brick walls, wood floors, warm lighting, marble tables, and modern fixtures. Mizuna's enchanting environment has been a welcoming refuge to locals and visitors alike. Our unpretentious and knowledgeable staff will make your entire dining experience memorable and fun. Since our opening in 1996, we have been consistently rated as one of Spokane's best restaurants by both local and regional newspapers and magazines. We have also been featured in Bon Appétit, Northwest Palate, and Northwest Best Places.

Ingredients

- 1 C. bulgur wheat
- 1 C. boiling water
- 2 Tbsp canola oil
- 1 onion, chopped
- 2 Tbsp garlic, chopped
- 4 C. crimini mushrooms, chopped
- 2 Tbsp soy sauce
- ¼ C. white wine
- ½ C. toasted hazelnuts
- 1 baguette
- 1 lb. extra firm tofu
- 1 Tbsp maple syrup
- 3 Tbsp balsamic vinegar
- 2 tsp Dijon mustard
- 2 Tbsp miso paste
- 1 Tbsp ground sage
- 1 tsp salt
- 2 tsp pepper
- 2 tsp garlic powder
- 1 Tbsp onion powder
- ¼ C. nutritional yeast
- 1 lb. package seitan, sliced

Directions

1. Preheat oven to 400°F.
2. Mix the water and bulgur in bowl, cover, and let sit for 20 minutes until most of the water is absorbed and bulgur is soft.
3. In a sauté pan, heat the canola oil over medium heat. Add the onions, garlic, and crimini mushrooms and sauté until soft. Deglaze the pan with the soy sauce and wine and then cook until most of the liquid is absorbed. Set aside to cool.
4. In a food processor, chop the hazelnuts into small pieces, set aside. Slice the baguette and pulse in a food processor to make bread crumbs, set aside.
5. Place the tofu, maple syrup, balsamic vinegar, Dijon, and miso paste into a food processor and mix until smooth. Pour into a large mixing bowl. Add the sage, salt, pepper, garlic powder, onion powder, and nutritional yeast.
6. In a food processor, pulse seitan until it is well ground and add to the large mixing bowl.
7. Add the chopped hazelnuts and bulgur wheat to mixing bowl.
8. In a food processor, pulse the sautéed mushroom mixture a few times, but do not puree, and add to mixing bowl.
9. Mix all ingredients together well.
10. Add about 2 C. of the bread crumbs and mix well, adding more breadcrumbs as needed. Mixture should be workable, not wet, but not so dry that it cracks when forming a patty.
11. Form the mixture into 12 (6-oz.) patties and sear both sides in a well-oiled pan on the stovetop until browned.
12. Transfer patties to a baking sheet and bake for about 10 minutes, or until center is hot.

214 North Howard Street

Mizuna

"We hope that your experience at Mizuna will inspire and enrich you. We are so thankful for all the incredible people who have come through our doors and the many regulars who have faithfully supported us over the years. You make our job easy!"
Mike Jones, Owner

Gorgonzola Pasta Salad

Monterey Café was opened in 2009 in downtown Spokane. As Spokane's only beach-style tiki bar, we specialize in fun! Our menu boasts specialty pizzas from the Wingman to the T-Rex, calzones, salads, nachos, pitas, wraps, and much more. With a full bar and karaoke six nights a week, there's something for everyone here!

1 lb. of penne pasta, cooked, drained, and chilled
2 C. blue cheese dressing
2 C. gorgonzola cheese, crumbled
1 C. parmesan cheese, grated
1 C. bacon, cooked crisp, crumbled
1 C. ham, diced
¼ C roasted red peppers, diced
salt and pepper, to taste
1 C. sharp cheddar cheese, grated

1. Place chilled pasta in a large bowl, add the blue cheese dressing and mix well.

2. Add gorgonzola crumbles and grated parmesan cheese and mix well.

3. Add the rest of ingredients except the grated cheddar cheese, mix well, and refrigerate for 1 to 2 hours.

4. Top with grated cheddar cheese and serve.

Monterey Café
9 North Washington Street

"When the Spokane weather has you down, stop in the Monterey Café for a slice of sunshine!"
Misty Straley, Manager

BREWERS WINGS

Northern Lights Brewing Co. was founded in October 1993 and was the vision of Mark Irvin, a Spokane native. In June 2002 the NLBC moved to its current location on East Trent Avenue in Spokane and began operating as a brewery and pub. Northern Lights Brewing Co. has become "Spokane's brewery" and is consistently voted as the best brewery in the area. It is a priority for NLBC to use local vendors and food producers, including local wineries.

1 lb. chicken wings
1½ C. Franks buffalo sandwich sauce
⅓ C. enchilada sauce
1 Tbsp minced garlic
1 tsp Aurora Borealis house spice or Cajun spice blend
1 Tbsp butter
2 tsp granulated garlic
1 Tbsp crushed red pepper flakes

1. Preheat oil in a fryer to 350°F or preheat oven to 350°F and fry or bake the chicken wings until cooked through. Time will vary depending on method.

2. In a medium sauté pan, heat the buffalo sauce, enchilada sauce, minced garlic, Aurora Borealis house spice, butter, granulated garlic, and crushed red pepper flakes.

3. When the sauce is bubbling, add the wings and toss until they are fully coated. Serve with your favorite dipping sauce.

Note: For a hotter sauce add more pepper flakes. For the hottest sauce add Dave's Insanity Sauce and more granulated garlic to balance the flavor.

NORTHERN LIGHTS BREWING CO.
1003 EAST TRENT AVENUE

"Working in a brewery is the best place for me. Creating great food with amazing beers is an exciting challenge every day."
Lane Truesdell, Executive Chef

CREAMY VEGAN MUSHROOM SOUP

Signature Tastes of SPOKANE

One World Café is dedicated to serving local, unprocessed food grown without chemicals and toxins. We are dedicated to eliminating waste in the food industry and giving all members of the community access to healthy, sustainable food. We do this by choosing an unconventional approach to addressing food insecurity without mass-produced industrial agriculture. It is unconventional because food is prepared in small batches with the seasons and served to patrons who choose their own portions of soups, salads, pizza, and desserts. Patrons are expected to pay a fair and respectable price for the food that they have eaten based on their personal circumstances.

¾ lb. of fresh mushrooms, sliced (local, wild morel mushrooms are best)
½ of 1 organic onion, diced (or white and light green park of one leek)
2 organic garlic cloves, minced
1 Tbsp vegan margarine or olive oil
3 C. organic vegetable broth
2 C. cooked potatoes, pureed
1 C. non-dairy yogurt
1 C. non-dairy milk
chopped fresh parsley
salt and pepper, to taste

1. In a large stock pot, sauté the mushrooms, onion, and garlic in the margarine or oil over medium heat for 3–5 minutes until the onions are translucent. Reduce heat to medium low and add the vegetable broth. Cover and simmer for 45 minutes.

2. Add the potato puree, non-dairy yogurt, and non-dairy milk, stirring well to combine. Simmer another 20–30 minutes, or until soup has thickened. Season with salt and pepper to taste. Sprinkle with parsley just before serving.

ONE WORLD CAFÉ
1804 EAST SPRAGUE AVENUE

"The One World concept is about local food, sustainability, partnerships, building community, reducing waste, and providing our customers with delicious, vibrant cuisine, and an exceptional dining experience where everyone "breaks bread" together. If you enjoy our food, atmosphere, and philosophy please tell a friend — word of mouth is our best advertising."
Janice Raschko, General Manager and Owner

FRENCH ONION SOUP

There are only two original Onion Bar & Grill's in the whole world, and they are right here in Spokane, Washington. It all started in 1978 when our daring young founder, Larry Brown, wanted to try a fun new idea for family and friends. First, demand that everything be made from scratch, by using only fresh, local, natural products to create fun original recipes. Second, have a great bar with highly trained "old school" adult beverage technicians. Third, combine all this with our legendary "No Problem" service in a family-friendly restaurant and The Onion as you know it today was born.

1½ lb. butter
13½ lb. sweet white onions, sliced
4½ lb. red onions, sliced
4½ C. sherry
1½ C. brandy
12 bay leaves
1 Tbsp fresh cracked black pepper
2 Tbsp dried thyme
18 oz. Minors beef base
2¼ gal. water
2 Tbsp Worcestershire sauce
grilled sourdough bread
shredded cheese of your choice

1. In a large, heavy-bottomed pot, melt the butter over medium heat and add the sliced onions. Cook slowly, stirring occasionally until they are caramelized, about 45–50 minutes.

2. Deglaze the pan with sherry and brandy.

3. Add the bay leaves, pepper, and thyme.

4. Add the beef base, water, and Worcestershire sauce, bring to a boil and let simmer, uncovered, for 15 minutes.

5. Place soup into shallow pans to cool.

6. To serve the soup, preheat broiler or set oven to 350°F. Reheat portions of the soup and place into oven-proof crocks, top with a slice of grilled sourdough bread and shredded cheese of your choice. Broil or bake until cheese is bubbly and golden brown.

Signature Tastes of SPOKANE

THE ONION BAR & GRILL
MULTIPLE LOCATIONS

"Our 'No Problem' mission of exceeding your expectations is as strong today as it was when it all began thirty-three years ago! You are the reason we are here and we really value your thoughts and comments! We are not happy unless you are."
Kenneth Belisle, President

TZATZIKI

Signature Tastes of SPOKANE

OPA! is Spokane's premier Mediterranean restaurant. Known for a warm and inviting atmosphere with friendly service, OPA has become one of Spokane's favorite restaurants. OPA prides itself on using the best ingredients possible while providing an excellent value to its customers. We hope you enjoy this recipe for our cool cucumber and Greek yogurt sauce. OPA!

2 C. plain Greek yogurt
1 large cucumber, peeled, seeded, shredded
2 garlic cloves, crushed
½ tsp salt
¼ tsp ground black pepper
¼ C. chopped fresh basil leaves

1. Line a fine sieve with two layers of cheese cloth and set over a bowl. Strain the yogurt for 2 hours, or until most of the water has drained out.

2. Press excess liquid out of the shredded cucumber with a paper towel. In a medium bowl, stir together the cucumber and strained yogurt. Mix in the garlic, salt, pepper, and basil. Chill for 1 to 2 hours.

Note: This Tzatziki sauce is an excellent accompaniment for both meat and as a salad dressing.

10411 NORTH NEWPORT HIGHWAY

OPA!

"Mediterranean food is all about family!"
slogan for OPA!

149

Spinach and Artichoke Dip

Pacific Avenue Pizza is a family-friendly full service restaurant and bar located in historic Browne's Addition. We specialize in gourmet pizza, sandwiches, and salads. We offer a full bar with beer, wine, and spirits and there are two patios for outside dining.

2 C. chopped spinach
2 ½ C. artichoke hearts, chopped
¼ C. chopped jalapeños
¼ C. mayonnaise
12 oz. cream cheese, softened
⅓ C. grated parmesan
⅓ C. grated mozzarella cheese
½ tsp garlic salt
1 Tbsp minced garlic
pita bread

1. Preheat oven to 425°F.

2. Combine all the ingredients in a large bowl and mix well. Spread evenly into a casserole dish and bake for 15 minutes, or until mixture is bubbling.

3. Toast pita in the oven for about 3–4 minutes and cut into wedges.

4. Serve spinach artichoke dip warm with wedges of pita bread for dipping.

"Pacific Avenue Pizza is a fun, friendly place serving Spokane's best pizza."
Darin Talloti, Owner

SPECIALTY HOME FRIES

The Perry Street Café is a small, locally-owned diner located in the South Perry District. We pride ourselves on serving homemade food that we prepare from scratch. The café specializes in serving breakfast and lunch, and our all-American dishes include Perry Street Café Specialty Home Fries, tasty deli "sammitches," and yummy dessert nibbles. Along with great tasting food at an affordable price, the Perry Street Café serves every dish with outstanding service, ensuring that each customer is satisfied and appreciated.

Signature Tastes of SPOKANE

4–6 large baking potatoes
1 large yellow onion, ½-inch dice
1 large bell pepper, ½-inch dice
Johnny's Seasoning Salt, to taste
¼ C. granulated garlic

1. Slice potatoes lengthwise and then into half-moon shapes about ⅜-inch thick (leave the skin on). Boil potatoes until just tender; be careful not to overcook. Run the potatoes under cold water to stop the cooking and set aside to cool.

2. Grease a hot pan or griddle set at 350°F with butter or margarine and toss in the potatoes, onions, and bell peppers. Season to taste with Johnny's Seasoning Salt and the granulated garlic and cook home fries until browned. Serve hot!

PERRY STREET CAFÉ
1002 SOUTH PERRY STREET

"Building good relationships with our customers has made the Perry Street Café a local favorite."
Geoff White, Owner

153

STICKY OAT BRAN MUFFINS

We purchased the bakery, which is located two blocks south of Whitworth University, in 2009 and we changed the name to Petit Chat Village Bakery. Our goal was to create a place for the local community to call their own and to spend time with friends and family. When we purchased the bakery, it was a small wholesale bread bakery only. We brought in our own at-home baking skills and soon realized we needed more room and more employees! We expanded to include a sit down area that offers coffee, croissants, pastries, and much more. Due to the wonderful support of the local community we are still here and the bakery has become more than we ever expected.

Muffin Pan Smear:
1 ⅓ C. brown sugar
½ C. canola oil
½ C. honey
½ C. corn syrup
2 Tbsp hot water

Batter:
2 C. wheat bran
1½ C. oats
1 C. whole-wheat flour
2 tsp baking soda
1 tsp baking powder
½ tsp salt
½ C. shredded carrots
½ C. dates, chopped
2 eggs
4 oz. pineapple tidbits
with juice
¾ C. milk
¾ C. plain yogurt
⅓ C. canola oil
½ C. honey
¼ C. molasses
1 tsp vanilla extract

1. Preheat oven to 350°F.
2. Using a mixer, cream all ingredients for the pan smear together. Smear 1–2 Tbsp of the mixture into the bottom of each muffin cup (large size) and then spray with non-stick cooking spray. Set aside.
3. Combine dry ingredients in a large bowl, including carrots and dates, and stir together.
4. Add all the wet ingredients to the bowl and whisk until incorporated. Mixture should be thick and resemble cooked oatmeal, if not, add a little more wheat bran.
5. Divide mixture evenly among muffin cups and bake muffins until a toothpick inserted in the center comes out clean, about 18–25 minutes.
6. Immediately place a wire cooling rack on top of the muffin tin and flip over to remove the muffins.

Note: Dried cranberries can be substituted for the dates and chunky applesauce can be used instead of pineapple. A ½ cup of chopped walnuts can be added, if preferred.

PETIT CHAT VILLAGE BAKERY

9910 NORTH WAIKIKI ROAD

"Our goal is to give you more than you expect and for you to feel like you are at home."
Kevin and Brenda Gerhart, Owners

CHICKEN POTSTICKERS

Located on Spokane's lower-South Hill, Picabu Bistro offers casual upscale dining in a bustling, friendly environment. The menu features an eclectic mix of Thai, American, Mexican, and Cajun-inspired favorites and a concise, quality selection of beer and wine.

Potsticker Filling:
1 lb. skinless, boneless chicken breast
4 Tbsp chopped green onion
⅓ C. fresh chopped cilantro
⅓ C. frozen kernel corn
2½ Tbsp ginger puree
1 Tbsp minced garlic
1 Tbsp soy sauce
2 Tbsp fresh lime juice

Potsticker Sauce:
2 C. soy sauce
1 C. water
⅔ C. sugar
1 C. white wine
⅓ C. rice wine vinegar
⅓ C. thinly sliced green onions

Potsticker Wrappers:
2½ C. unbleached all-purpose flour
½ C. corn starch
½ tsp salt
water

Garnish:
Black and white sesame seeds

Potsticker Filling:
1. Using a food processor, pulse the chicken a few times to grind and transfer half the mixture to a mixing bowl. Add the green onion and cilantro to the food processor and pulse a few times to combine with the remaining chicken. Transfer everything to the mixing bowl and add the corn, ginger puree, garlic, soy sauce, and lime juice and mix well.

Potsticker Sauce:
1. Place the soy sauce, water, sugar, white wine, and rice wine vinegar in a sauce pan and bring to a light boil, turn down heat and simmer for 15 minutes. Cool and garnish with sliced green onions.

Potsticker Wrappers:
1. Place flour, corn starch, and salt into the bowl of a stand mixer. Pour in a small amount of water and turn the mixer on the lowest setting. With the mixer running, continue to pour water in very slowly until dough forms. The dough should be firm but pliable.
2. Rest the dough on a cutting board covered with a damp cloth for 30 minutes.
3. Roll out dough on a well-floured surface to about ⅛-inch thickness. To form wrappers, cut dough into 4-inch circles.

Finish the Potstickers:
1. Place 1 Tbsp of potsticker filling into the center of each wrapper and fold over to form a half-moon shape. Pinch the edges to seal.
2. Heat 1 Tbsp of canola oil in a non-stick pan over medium-high heat and add 6–8 of the potstickers at a time and cook until the bottoms are golden brown. Add about ⅓ C. of water, cover, and steam about 5 minutes, or until filling is cooked through.
3. Plate the potstickers on top a bed of mixed greens and garnish with a sprinkle of black and white sesame seeds and serve with the potsticker sauce.

PICABU BISTRO
901 WEST FOURTEENTH AVENUE

"We have a small menu but a huge variety of flavors."
Jane Edwards, Owner

CHAMPAGNE TORTELLINI WITH JUMBO PRAWNS

Walk through our front doors and you will know that you are in for something special. Our natural log interior and Rocky Mountain granite fireplaces take you back to a much simpler time when "comfort food" was a staple. Our chefs create just that — comfort food with a twist. An open kitchen allows our guests to watch their brick-oven pizzas or their beautifully presented salads being prepared right before them. Our knowledgeable staff will take extra special care of you in our warm atmosphere, where you are sure to come back time and again.

1 oz. extra virgin olive oil
1 tsp minced garlic
2 Tbsp unsalted butter
5 jumbo tiger prawns, peeled and deveined
1 Tbsp sea salt
2 lemon wedges
½ C. champagne
½ C. heavy cream
1 (10-oz.) package tri-color cheese tortellini, pre-cooked
¾ C. shredded parmesan cheese
¼ of 1 yellow bell pepper, julienne
¼ of 1 green bell pepper, julienne
¼ of 1 red bell pepper, julienne

Garnish:
2 lemon wedges
3 whole chives

1. In a medium sauce pan, heat the olive oil, garlic, and butter over high heat and sauté until butter is melted.

2. Add the prawns, sea salt, and lemon wedges and cook until shrimp are slightly underdone, 1–2 minutes. Deglaze the pan with champagne and allow the alcohol to cook off.

3. Next add the heavy cream, tortellini, parmesan cheese, and peppers. Turn heat down to medium low and stir frequently until the tortellini is heated through and the champagne sauce has thickened. Remove both lemon wedges and place ingredients into a pasta dish and garnish with fresh lemon wedges and chives.

PROSPECTOR'S BAR & GRILL
12611 NORTH DIVISION STREET

"Our staff is here to serve you and make your experience wonderful. Come see why we are fast becoming the region's favorite place to enjoy a meal out. We are proudly locally owned and operated."
Dave Blair, Owner

SPLIT LENTIL SAUCE

Owner Almaz Ainuu was born and raised in Ethiopia. Currently she resides in Spokane Valley with her husband and is living her dream of having an Ethiopian restaurant, thus introducing her culture and cuisine to the wonderful people of Spokane. Ethiopian dining is a unique experience where the meal is traditionally served in a communal setting and the food is shared on a single platter. The platter is covered with injera, a flat bread, similar to a crepe but with a spongy texture. Ethiopian cooking offers an abundance of vegetarian dishes but beef, lamb, and chicken are just as popular.

*2 C. split red lentils
6 C. of hot water
1½ C. vegetable oil
2 C. red onion, diced
½ C. berberé (substitute
½ C. cayenne pepper
or turmeric*)
1 Tbsp chopped
fresh ginger
1 tsp chopped garlic
¼ tsp cumin
1 tsp salt*

**use turmeric for
mild spice*

1. Rinse the lentils and set aside.

2. Pour the 6 C. of water into a pot and bring to a boil, hold at a simmer.

3. In a medium pot, heat the oil over medium heat and add the onions. Cook for 5 minutes or until lightly browned, stirring frequently.

4. Add the berberé (or cayenne pepper or turmeric) and the rinsed lentils and cook for 10 minutes, stirring occasionally. You may adjust the quantities of berberé or cayenne to taste.

5. Add the ginger, garlic, cumin, and salt and stir for 1 minute, then add the 6 C. of simmering water. Cook for 20 minutes, stirring occasionally, until mixture is thick. Let cool for 5 minutes before serving.

QUEEN OF SHEBA
621 WEST MALLON AVENUE

"We'd like to thank our customers for all of their support. We are proud to be the first to bring the authentic foods of Ethiopia to Spokane!"
Almaz Ainuu, Owner

Open Rocket BAKERY

Coffee
Pastries

Come in, and Blast Off!

COFFEE

	8oz	12oz	16oz	20oz
ESPRESSO	1.5			
AMERICANO	1.75	1.85	2.00	2.20
CAFFE LATTE	2.60	2.95	3.30	3.65
CAPPUCCINO	2.60	2.95	3.30	
CAFFE MOCHA	2.70	3.25	3.60	3.95
CAFFE GENERRA	3.00	3.35	3.70	4.05
BREVE	2.90	3.25	3.60	3.95
CARAMEL & WHITE CHOC. LATTE & MOCHA	3.00	3.30	3.60	3.90
DRIP COFFEE	1.75	1.50	1.75	2.00
'N HOUSE REFILLS!	25	35	40	50
CHAI	2.50	2.85	3.15	3.40
YERBA MATTE	1.70	1.75	2.20	2.45
MATTE LATTE	2.60	2.85	3.05	3.30
HOT CHOCOLATE	1.70	1.95	2.20	2.45
ITALIAN SODAS		1.95	2.20	2.45
JET TEA		2.70	3.20	3.70
COMETS		3.35	3.60	3.95
TEA: HOT & ICED 1.70				

Extras
ESPRESSO SHOT 50¢
FLAVOR 20¢
WHIPPED CREAM,
ORANGE PEEL
DILETTANTE CHOCOLATE 40¢
RICE OR SOY MILK

THE ROCKET NOW HAS

1/2 off per coffee & per 16 box
14.99

JoinRocket.com

BAKERY

CINNAMON ROLLS 2.25
CARAMEL PECAN ROLLS 2.45
BLUEBERRY AND BOYSENBERRY DANISH 2.55

SCONES 1.85 MUFFINS 1.75 COOKIES 1.75/1.95
DESSERTS 3.50 SWEET BREADS 1.85

BARS: RASPBERRY OAT LEMON BLUEBERRY
PEACH APPLE OAT NANAIMO 2.55
• PUMPKIN BARS • BROWNIES • CARAMEL BROWNIES

BAGELS

BAGELS 1.09 FLAVORED BAGELS 1.09
TOPPINGS: CREAM CHEESE • PLAIN OR NON-FAT 1.15
FLAVORED 1.15 BLUEBERRY, GARLIC
RAISIN HONEY WALNUT, VEGGIE, SMOKED SALMON,
MARTINI OLIVE, JALAPENO-CHEDDAR, SUNDRIED TOMATO PEST

Breakfast Bagel 4.25
FLUFFY EGGS, CHEDDAR & CANADIAN BACON

CHOCOLATE ZUCCHINI MUFFINS

Welcome to Rocket Bakery! We're a locally owned bakery and coffeehouse with nine neighborhood locations in the Spokane area. Since 1992, we've been making all of our baked goods with the most wholesome scratch ingredients, and we brew some of best joe and specialty drinks around. So whether you're looking for a great latte, scones for your next office party, or wholesale items for your business, come on in. Relax and enjoy the local flavor.

2½ C. grated zucchini
1 C. applesauce
1 C. molasses
¾ C. brown sugar
1 egg white
1¾ tsp vanilla extract
1½ tsp baking powder
1½ tsp baking soda
3¼ C. flour
¾ C. cocoa powder

1. Preheat oven to 350°F.

2. In a large bowl, mix zucchini, applesauce, molasses, and brown sugar together.

3. Add the egg white and vanilla extract.

4. Sift the baking powder, baking soda, flour, and cocoa powder together, then add to wet mixture and mix thoroughly.

5. Pour batter into greased muffin tins and bake for about 15–20 minutes.

"This was a favorite recipe we made when we first opened and it's since been retired, but it is still delicious!"
Jeff and Julia Postlewait, Owners

ROCKET BAKERY
MULTIPLE LOCATIONS

QUINOA BRUSSELS SPROUTS

Located in the heart of Spokane's South Hill neighborhood, Rocket Market has spent the last decade providing specialty foods, including wine, produce, bakery, cheeses, meat coffee, and flowers. Our bistro, featuring local chef Shilo Pierce, specializes in fresh modern food that uses local ingredients whenever possible. We also take great pride in being a local business that purchases food from over fifty local purveyors.

3 C. Brussels sprouts, trimmed and quartered
½ C. olive oil, divided
1 large orange, halved
1 lemon, halved
1 shallot, minced
1½ C. of quinoa, cooked according to package directions
salt and pepper, to taste

1. Preheat oven to 375°F.

2. Combine Brussels sprouts with ¼ C. of olive oil, juice of half the lemon, and juice of half the orange, and roast on a sheet pan for 15–20 minutes, or until Brussels sprouts are crispy and browned. Set aside and cool.

3. In a bowl, stir the Brussels sprouts together with the quinoa, juice of half of the lemon, juice of half of the orange, the remaining ¼ C. of olive oil, and the minced shallot. Add salt and pepper to taste. Serve at room temperature or chilled.

ROCKET MARKET
726 EAST FORTY-THIRD STREET

"Our reason for existence is to provide local, wholesome food and expert advice on all aspects of wine, food, and its preparation."
Alan Shepherd, Managing Partner

CHICKEN FIESTA SALAD WITH CHIPOTLE-LIME DRESSING

The Satellite Diner first opened its doors in February of 1998 and quickly became a Spokane institution. Open for 21 hours a day, you can get breakfast, lunch, dinner, or anything in between including some of the best hand-crafted cocktails on Earth.

Chipotle-Lime Dressing:
1 package ranch dressing mix, prepared according to directions
¼ C. chipotle Tabasco sauce
2 Tbsp lime juice

Salad:
2 C. salad greens
2 oz. diced green onion
2 oz. diced roasted red pepper
3 oz. shredded cheddar cheese
2 bacon strips, cooked crisp, crumbled
1 boneless, skinless grilled chicken breast, diced
salt and pepper, to taste

1. Mix all ingredients for the dressing together and refrigerate.

2. In a large bowl, assemble salad greens, green onion, roasted red pepper, and cheddar cheese. Top with crumbled bacon and diced chicken. Add salt and pepper to taste. Serve with chipotle-lime dressing.

SATELLITE DINER
425 WEST SPRAGUE AVENUE

"The Satellite Diner: We revolve around you!"
slogan for Satellite Diner

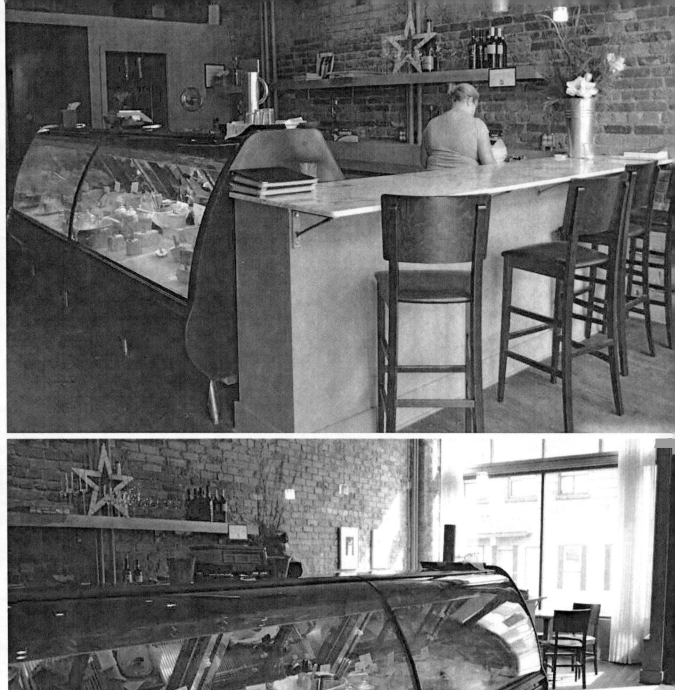

HOW TO CRAFT A CHEESE PLATE

Saunders Cheese Market is in the downtown SoDo District, just north of Vino! A Wine Shop on Washington. Open for five years, Saunders carries a wide variety of domestic and imported artisanal cheeses, as well as accompaniments to spice up any cheese plate. We also offer cheese boards and carry a small variety of wines, or bring in your own bottle for a reasonable corkage fee. With additional hours during the holidays, our hours are Wednesday and Thursday 11 am–5 pm, Friday 10 am–7 pm, and Saturday 10 am–5 pm. Here we offer some tips on how to create the perfect cheese plate at home to impress guests, spoil your family, or enjoy with your favorite wine.

1. Purchasing: The cheeses you select should be cut fresh. Properly cut and cared for cheeses will always taste better and look better than cheeses that have been indifferently cared for. Purchase your cheeses as close as possible to when you plan to serve them; this ensures that you will have the greatest possible quality. For a cheese plate, plan on approximately one ounce of each cheese per person, depending on whether you will be serving it alone or with other cheeses. For four people, this translates to a quarter pound of each cheese.

2. Serving: Cheese should be served at room temperature to allow the flavors to really shine. Generally it takes about an hour for cheeses to reach room temperature. You can serve the cheese in wedges; if you choose to do so, have a sharp knife for each cheese. When arranging the cheeses, be sure to serve mildest to strongest. This ensures that no cheese is overshadowed.

3. Selecting: The following list provides a guide for selecting cheeses. Choose one type of cheese from each category for a balanced plate of five cheeses. Nuts, meats, olives, and fruits make excellent partners with any of them.

Building the Cheese Plate:
1. Soft: Brillat Savarin, Up in Smoke, Cana de Oveja, Teleme, Robiola
2. Mild: Mahon, Abbaye de Belloc, Wagon Wheel, Carmody, Tomme de Savoie
3. Hard: Piave, Roncal, Cabot Cheddar, Pecorino, Garrotxa,
4. Washed Rind: Red Hawk, Ardrahan, Grayson, Taleggio, Oma
5. Blue: Flora Nelle, Stilton, Rossini, Valdeon, Roquefort

SAUNDERS CHEESE MARKET

210 SOUTH WASHINGTON STREET

"Cheese is milk's leap towards immortality."
Clifton Fadiman

Fireman's Steak Sandwich

Located in the Northwest corner of Spokane, Shan's is a neighborhood bar and grill that serves a large menu which includes sandwiches, burgers, steak, and pasta dishes. We also have a great appetizer menu to enjoy when meeting family or friends. We provide a relaxing atmosphere and excellent food that is enjoyed by people of all ages. Shan's is also a great place to enjoy your favorite sporting events on any of our large TV's. We have a great selection of beer on tap plus liquor from the only full bar in the Indian Trail neighborhood.

1 C. mayonnaise
½ C. chipotle chilis in adobo, finely chopped
4 (8-oz.) sirloin steaks
4 slices pepper jack cheese
1 Tbsp oil
1 C. sliced white onion
½ C. sliced jalapeños
4 eggs
4 hoagie buns

1. Add the chopped chipotle chilis to the mayonnaise and mix thoroughly. Set aside.

2. Grill steaks to desired doneness, slice into ¼-inch strips and place back on the grill. Put a slice of pepper jack cheese on each steak to melt.

3. While steaks are grilling, heat oil in a sauté pan and cook onions and jalapeños over medium heat until onions are soft. Set aside.

4. In another sauté pan, fry the eggs to medium hard.

5. Warm the hoagie buns on the grill.

6. Spread some of the chipotle mayonnaise on each bun, place the steaks on the bun and top with the onions and jalapeños. Add one egg on top of each sandwich. Garnish top of egg with a drizzle of the chipotle mayonnaise.

8801 North Indian Trail Road

Shan's Grill

"Please join us for your next evening out."
Shannon Powell, Owner and General Manager

APPLE FRITTER CAKE

The Skyway Café is located at Felts Field in Spokane. Breakfast is served all day and all meals have huge portions. Nothing beats watching small planes and helicopters land and take off while you enjoy your heaping mound of hash browns. This is a great place to take friends and family for a relaxing Sunday brunch. The décor is aircraft themed--model planes hang from the ceiling and plane art hangs throughout.

Apple Fritter Cake:
3 cinnamon rolls from
Skyway Café or
1 loaf of cinnamon
raisin bread, cubed
1 (20-oz.) can of
apple pie filling
1 Tbsp vanilla extract
4 eggs
2 C. milk
½ C. brown sugar
½ C. granulated sugar
½ tsp cinnamon
½ C. butter, melted

Glaze:
1 C. butter, melted
2 Tbsp milk
1 Tbsp vanilla extract
2 C. confectioner's sugar

1. Preheat oven to 350°F.

2. Grease a 9x13-inch baking pan and set aside.

3. Spread half of the cubed cinnamon rolls or bread in the bottom of the baking pan.

4. Spoon the apple pie filling evenly on top.

5. Place the other half of the cubed cinnamon rolls or bread over the apple filling.

6. In a bowl, mix together the vanilla extract, eggs, milk, both sugars, cinnamon, and the melted butter and pour evenly over top. Bake for 45 minutes, or until golden brown. Set aside to cool.

7. To make the glaze, stir all the ingredients together and drizzle over the cooled cake.

SKYWAY CAFÉ
6105 EAST RUTTER AVENUE

"We'd love to make you breakfast!"
Becky Eddy, Baker

PULLED PORK SANDWICHES

Sonnenberg's Market & Deli was established in 1984 when Clyde Sonnenberg bought the business. The store has been on the corner of Sprague and Helena since 1891 making it the oldest continuously-running market in town. Sonnenberg's has seventy feet of meat service counters including the deli and we provide a large selection of meats, custom cutting, and wild game processing for sausage and jerky as well as a grocery market with fresh vegetables and everything you need to make the perfect meal. Sonnenberg's also caters events including large business picnics/lunches, weddings, and private parties. Although our New York Style Italian sausage has been our most popular item for many years, this recipe for pulled pork sandwiches has proven to be very popular and is one of the most requested for events.

1 (6-lb.) pork shoulder
roast, bone-in
(Boston butt)
¼ C. light brown sugar
¼ C. paprika
1 Tbsp smoked paprika
3 Tbsp kosher salt
2 Tbsp ground
black pepper
1 tsp cayenne pepper
2 tsp dry mustard
1 tsp onion powder
1 tsp garlic powder
1 tsp chipotle
chili powder
1 tsp cinnamon

1. Using a knife, score pork shoulder in a crisscross pattern on the top and bottom about ¼-inch in depth.
2. Mix all the dry ingredients together to make the rub, measure out about half of the rub and reserve the other half for another use. Massage the rub all over the pork, make sure to get it down into the slits.
3. In a crock pot set on low heat, cook the pork shoulder, fat side up, for 8 hours.
4. When the pork is done, remove from crock pot and set aside to cool. Drain and reserve the cooking juices. Separate the fat from juice by putting it in the freezer; the fat will float to the top, skim fat off the top and discard.
5. When pork is cool enough to handle, pull the pork into pieces with your hands, discard large pieces of fat and bone. Pour about 1 C. of reserved juices over the top. If not serving right away, refrigerate and reheat in a pan just before serving. Serve on small rolls or hamburger buns with your favorite barbeque sauce and coleslaw.

"The Oldest Meat Market in Town! Serving Spokane since 1891."
slogan for Sonnenberg's

SOULFUL CHICKEN ARTICHOKE SOUP

Our soups and spirits lounge has been a welcoming downtown Spokane lunch destination for over eleven years. We serve delicious homemade soups Monday through Friday as well as a tasty selection of hot and cold sandwiches and salads. Don't miss our world famous beer bread – baked fresh everyday! We make about twenty-five different soup flavors throughout the week so check with us for our soup schedule and daily chef specials too! By night, Soulful literally transforms into the Spirits Lounge. The lights dim and the candles flicker and we offer a great selection of beer, wine, and cocktails. For your entertainment, we have live music on Thursdays and Fridays as well as specialty DJ's throughout the week.

2 Tbsp olive oil
2–3 C. tightly packed fresh spinach (or 5 oz. frozen)
2 C. carrots, small dice
2 C. celery, small dice
2 C. yellow onions, small dice
2 C. artichoke hearts, diced
2 Tbsp garlic, minced
⅛ C. dried basil
2 Tbsp dried thyme
2 Tbsp salt
1 Tbsp pepper
2 C. diced chicken, cooked
2 qt. water
1 qt. heavy cream
4 C. parmesan cheese, shredded and sprinkled with corn starch
¼ C. corn starch + ¼ C. water
croutons

1. Heat olive oil in a large non-stick pot over medium-high heat and add the carrots, celery, onion, spinach, artichokes, garlic, basil, and thyme. Sauté until the vegetables are softened; then add the salt and pepper.
2. Add the diced chicken, water, and heavy cream and bring to a boil over high heat, stirring frequently. Once the liquid boils, turn heat down to a simmer and cook until vegetables are very soft, (particularly the carrots and celery), then turn off the heat.
3. Slowly stir in the corn starch-coated parmesan cheese, about ½ C. at a time, making sure all of the cheese has melted before adding more.
4. To thicken the soup, make a slurry by mixing ¼ C. corn starch with a ¼ C. of water and stir until smooth. Add slurry to soup and stir for about 1 minute. If desired, add the same amount of corn starch slurry to thicken the soup to your preference. If you have time, leave the soup in a crock pot for about 4 hours holding a temperature of 160–180°F. Garnish with shredded parmesan cheese and croutons. Enjoy!

SOULFUL SOUPS AND SPIRITS
117 NORTH HOWARD STREET

"Come in and enjoy our comfortable, fun little space! Cheers!"
RJ Portmann and Julles Messmann, Owners

PROSCIUTTO PIZZA

Coming to the South Perry District is like stepping into a small town. This quirky little neighborhood located southeast of downtown Spokane is home to some of the most creative and friendly people in town. We are so proud to exist here among the other locally-owned businesses that comprise this flourishing district. The neighborhood seamlessly blends the charm of its historic buildings with a forward-thinking community. Like the neighborhood, our prosciutto pizza exudes incredible flavor and uniqueness. We strive to create delicious pizzas that satisfy without overwhelming – that push the bounds of typical American pizza while still providing its classic comfort. This pie does exactly that!

Signature Tastes of SPOKANE

Pizza Dough:
1 ½ C. flour
1 tsp salt
¾ tsp active dry yeast
½ C. lukewarm water
(plus more as needed)
1 Tbsp olive oil

Prosciutto Pizza:
12 oz. pizza dough
1 Tbsp + 1 tsp olive oil
¾ C. whole milk
mozzarella, shredded
4 slices prosciutto,
finely chopped
⅔ C. mascarpone cheese
1 C. arugula
12 grape tomatoes,
halved

Pizza Dough:

1. Stir together the dry ingredients, including yeast, in a large bowl. Add the water and olive oil and stir until the dough starts to come together.

2. Place dough on a lightly floured surface and shape into ball. Knead the dough for 2 minutes, or until smooth and place in a lightly oiled bowl and turn the dough to coat. Cover with plastic wrap and let rise in a warm place for 1 or 2 hours, until the dough has doubled in size.

3. Once the dough has risen, punch down the dough to release any air pockets. Reshape the dough into a ball and set it on a lightly floured surface and let it rest, covered loosely with plastic wrap, for 20 more minutes.

Prosciutto Pizza:

1. Insert a pizza stone into the bottom ⅓ of the oven and preheat oven to 500°F.

2. Stretch pizza dough to ⅛-inch thickness. Place the dough onto floured bottom of a baking sheet or a pizza peel.

3. Brush the olive oil over the dough leaving a ½-inch perimeter dry for the crust.

4. Cover olive oil layer with shredded mozzarella and sprinkle the prosciutto overtop, then drop the mascarpone by spoonfuls around the pizza.

5. Slide the pizza directly onto the pizza stone or place the entire baking sheet in the oven if you don't have a stone. Bake for 10–12 minutes or until crust is golden brown and cheese is melted. Arrange the arugula and tomato halves evenly over the pizza and serve.

SOUTH PERRY PIZZA
1011 SOUTH PERRY STREET

"I love my pizza so much, in fact, that I have come to believe in my delirium that my pizza might actually love me, in return. I am having a relationship with this pizza, almost an affair."
Elizabeth Gilbert, Eat, Pray, Love

The Steam Plant Grill opened in 1999 and is the vision of Spokane's historic renovation experts, Ron and Julie Wells and their business partners and sons, Gage and Spencer Stromberg. Having completed work on the award-winning renovation of the building, they wanted to showcase the art and architecture by adding a restaurant with views of the catwalks, pipes, and boilers. The original equipment of the Steam Plant is found throughout the Steam Plant Grill, leaving no doubt what the original purpose of the building was. The menu is loaded with delicious items made from scratch and composed of many local ingredients. Several menu items also feature the award-winning beer that is brewed on premise.

1 lb. U-10 dry-pack scallops
1 C. flour
2 oz. olive oil
2 oz. sliced shallots
2 oz. chopped garlic
4 oz. roasted red peppers
4 oz. roasted yellow peppers
4 oz. clam broth or shell stock
2 Tbsp garam masala
4 oz. heavy cream
12 oz. linguine noodles, cooked and drained
3 oz. shredded parmesan cheese
1 oz. sliced green onion

1. Dust the scallops in flour. Heat the olive oil in a sauté pan over high heat and add scallops when oil is very hot. Brown both sides of scallops, approximately 1–2 minutes per side. Remove scallops to a plate lined with paper towels.

2. In the same pan, add the shallots, garlic, and peppers to the oil and sauté for 2 minutes over medium heat.

3. Add the clam broth and garam masala, reduce by half.

4. Add the cream and reduce until sauce is thick enough to coat the back of a spoon.

5. Return the scallops to the pan, toss in the sauce to coat and then add the cooked linguini, tossing frequently until pasta is hot.

6. Divide among two bowls and garnish with the parmesan cheese and green onions.

STEAM PLANT GRILL
159 SOUTH LINCOLN STREET

"There's no place like it on Earth! The Steam Plant Grill is a steam plant built in the early 1900s renovated into an industrially chic restaurant and brewery. Catwalks overhead, old boilers you can dine inside, a smokestack over 200 feet high, award-winning microbrews crafted on premise, and an amazing menu all come together to make this locally-owned landmark a must-see experience."
Tim Denniston, General Manager

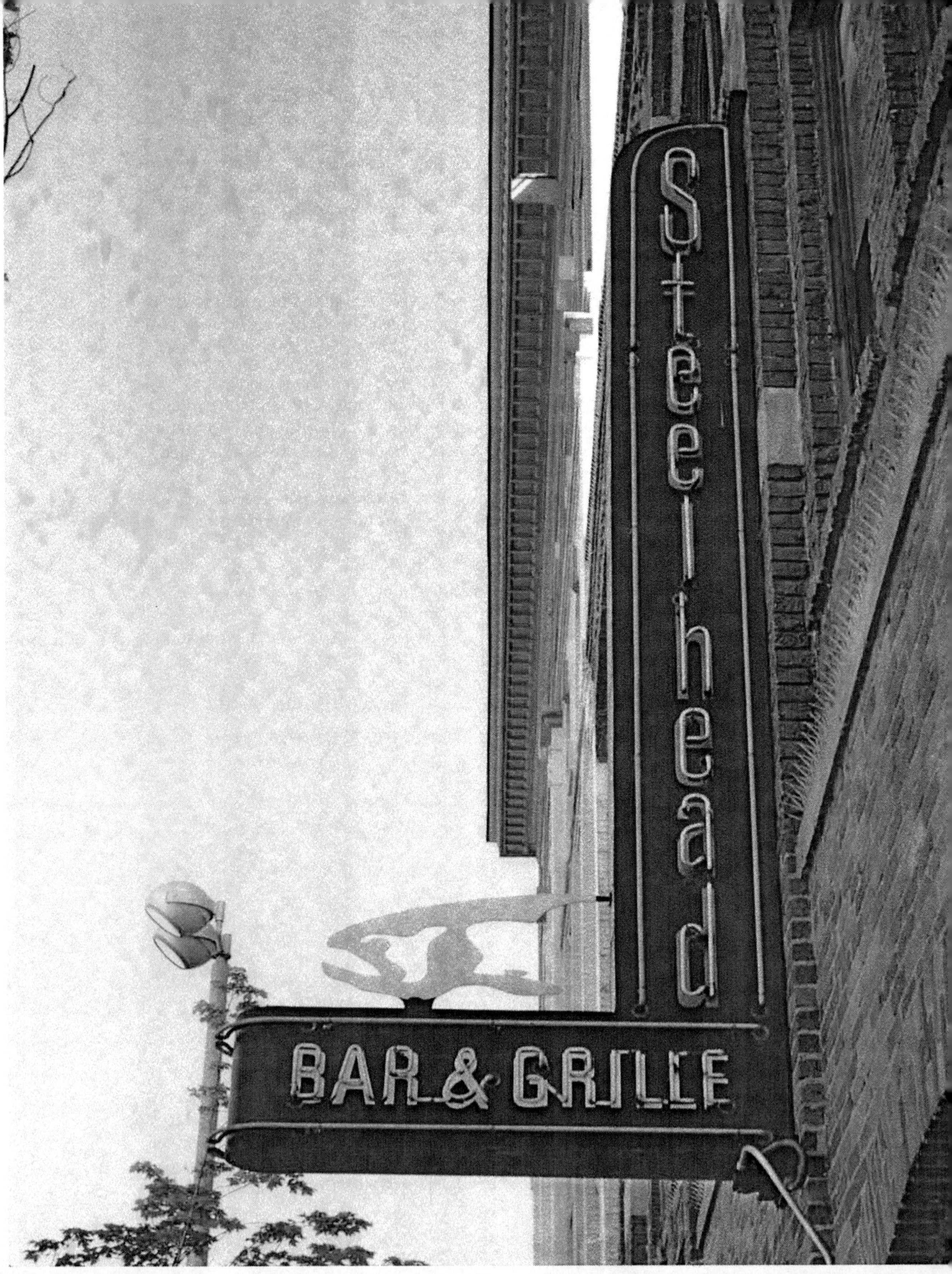
Steelhead
BAR & GRILLE

CHAMPAGNE HALIBUT

Located in the heart of downtown Spokane, Steelhead Bar & Grille combines historic industrial Spokane with contemporary accents, creating an atmosphere that is unique and inviting. The architectural artwork of the brushed steel bar, hammered copper fireplace, and warm, textured walls that include crushed marble work together to make Steelhead a place you will want to visit and stay a while. With a full bar, affordable menu, carefully selected beer and wine list, we have a little something for everyone.

2 (6-oz.) pieces of halibut
2 Tbsp extra virgin olive oil
1 Tbsp fresh minced garlic
4 oz. champagne
4 oz. heavy cream
1 oz. toasted slivered almonds (or 1 oz. slivered red peppers)
salt and pepper, to taste

1. Lightly salt and pepper both sides of the pieces of halibut and set aside.
2. Pour the extra virgin olive oil into a sauté pan and heat over medium-high heat. When the oil is hot, add the minced garlic and cook for 2 minutes, stirring.
3. Add the halibut to the pan and turn the halibut over when the bottom third of the fish is opaque, approximately 2 minutes.
4. Carefully add the champagne and the heavy cream and cook for 3–5 minutes, stirring occasionally until the sauce is thickened and the halibut is opaque and firm to the touch (do not overcook).
5. When the fish is done, immediately remove it from the pan and plate it. If necessary, continue to cook the sauce until it is thick. Liberally spoon the sauce over the halibut and garnish the dish with toasted almond slivers or red pepper slivers. We recommend serving this dish with asparagus or broccolini spears.

STEELHEAD BAR & GRILLE

218 NORTH HOWARD STREET

"We are a locally-owned restaurant and pub that features American cuisine with a Northwest twist."
Greg Reynolds, General Manager

CUCUMBER CILANTRO MARTINI

Stix Bar and Grill is proudly owned and operated by QoL Restaurant Group who also owns Twigs Bistro and Martini Bar. Prepare for a unique dining experience that is casual yet memorable. Visit any of our locations and you will experience the perfect ambiance, making for a warm and inviting atmosphere with food that will tantalize a variety of palates. Our newest northside hotspot serves up innovative first courses, unique hand-crafted cocktails, delicious burgers and sandwiches, mouth watering stone oven pizzas, and much more.

2 oz. Finlandia vodka
½ oz. triple sec
3 oz. white cranberry juice
1 lime, halved
2 cucumber slices
handful of fresh cilantro

1. Add ice to a cocktail shaker and muddle the lime, cucumber slices, and cilantro.

2. Add the vodka, triple sec, and white cranberry juice. Shake well and strain into a cocktail glass.

STIX BAR & GRILL
9820 NORTH NEVADA STREET

"I truly believe in supporting local businesses as much as possible."
Karen Blackwell, Proprietor

185

TOMATO BRUSCHETTA

Walt MacDuff is the executive chef of the Sundance Bistro and his wife Victoria is a gourmet baker. In addition to Walt and Victoria personally preparing and serving each meal, their sons frequent the Bistro to learn the family business. Excellent authentic Italian cuisine and scrumptious desserts with quality service is what you can expect every time you visit the Bistro. There is a full bar which is available not only to restaurant guests but also to golfers at the nearby Sundance Golf Course. Foodies can visit the Sundance Bistro all year long, so for the best Italian cuisine in Spokane, try the Sundance Bistro.

Signature Tastes of SPOKANE

Balsamic Glaze:
1 C. balsamic vinegar
2 Tbsp brown sugar
1 Tbsp soy sauce

Bruschetta:
3 medium tomatoes,
¼-inch dice
½ C. red onion,
¼-inch dice
½ C. minced garlic
½ C. fresh chopped basil
salt and pepper, to taste

Crostini:
1 loaf of crusty bread,
sliced ¼-inch thick
olive oil
grated parmesan cheese
chopped fresh parsley

Garnish:
¼ C. balsamic glaze
grated parmesan cheese
chopped fresh parsley

Balsamic Glaze:
1. Combine balsamic vinegar, brown sugar, and soy sauce in a small sauce pan and bring to a boil. Reduce heat to low and simmer until thick and syrupy, about 20 minutes. Remove from heat and let cool.

Bruschetta:
1. Combine tomatoes, onion, garlic, and basil in a bowl, mix well and season to taste with salt and pepper. Set aside for at least 1 hour to let flavors blend.

Crostini:
1. Preheat oven to 400°F.
2. Brush sliced bread with olive oil, place slices on a baking sheet, sprinkle with shredded parmesan cheese and chopped parsley and bake for 5 minutes.

Assembly:
1. Place approximately 1 Tbsp of bruschetta topping on each crostini, drizzle balsamic glaze over the top, sprinkle with more grated parmesan cheese and chopped parsley.

SUNDANCE BISTRO
9725 NORTH NINE MILE ROAD

"A world without tomatoes is like a string quartet without violins."
Laurie Colwin

187

YAKISOBA

Come visit one of Spokane's finest restaurants serving authentic Japanese cuisine. Sushi.com brings the world of fresh fish right to you! Whether it is tuna from Hawaii or rare white salmon from Korea, the delicate fillets are flown in fresh daily, artfully flaked, and placed on a small pillar of cooked rice. If sushi isn't your green cup of tea, there are other excellent choices of teriyaki, sukiyaki, and tempura.

Signature Tastes of SPOKANE

1 Tbsp soy bean oil or other oil
¼ lb. rib eye steak or chicken breast, thinly sliced
2 C. cabbage, shredded
¼ C. onion, thinly sliced
¼ C. carrots, shredded
½ C. broccoli florets
1 C. white mushrooms, thinly sliced
pinch of hon dashi (can substitute a pinch of a crushed bouillon cube)
pinch of black pepper
4 oz. yakisoba noodles
1 tsp yakisoba sauce
½ tsp soy sauce

1. Heat the oil in a wok set over medium-high heat. Add the meat and quickly stir-fry 1–2 minutes until well browned.

2. Add all of the vegetables and stir-fry for 1 minute then add the hon dashi and black pepper.

3. Add the yakisoba noodles and the yakisoba sauce and stir, cook for 1 minute. Add the soy sauce and cook until beef or chicken are cooked as desired and vegetables are still crisp.

SUSHI.COM
430 WEST MAIN AVENUE

"The fine art of Japanese food arrangement shines at Sushi.com as each dish is creatively presented with simple style and design. If you like delicious, fresh sushi—don't miss Sushi.com!"
Hannah Lee, Owner

The Swinging Doors was established in May of 1981 under the name The Swinging Doors Tavern. Owners Bob and Barb Materne turned a small pizza parlor into a huge restaurant that now offers the best sports viewing in town. Although the front and back doors are no longer the saloon-style swinging doors and the country feel is somewhat gone, the name is still synonymous with great food, large portions, and friendly service.

2 ½ lb. ground beef
⅓ C. finely diced onions
½ C. ketchup
¼ tsp salt
¼ tsp pepper
¾ C. Heinz 57 sauce
1 egg, beaten
⅔ C. Japanese bread crumbs
½ Tbsp parsley flakes

1. Preheat oven to 350°F.

2. Mix all ingredients together in a large bowl and pack tightly into a loaf pan.

3. Bake until the internal temperature reaches 155°F with no pink spots, about 45 minutes to 1 hour.

4. Slice into ¾-inch slices and serve with mashed potatoes and brown gravy.

THE SWINGING DOORS
1018 WEST FRANCIS AVENUE

"The Swinging Doors is a family-owned business that has been a part of the Spokane community for over thirty years. Our restaurant offers huge portions and a wonderful atmosphere second to none in the Spokane area."
Bob and Barb Materne, Owners

Bhindi Masala

Signature Tastes of SPOKANE

1 tsp coriander seeds
4 whole cloves
12 whole peppercorns
½ stick of cinnamon
1 large cardamom
pod (black)
2 Tbsp oil
1 tsp cumin seeds
½ large onion, sliced
2 garlic cloves, minced
½ Tbsp turmeric powder
chili powder, to taste
salt, to taste
1-inch piece of fresh
ginger, finely minced
1 lb. okra, sliced
crosswise
2 Tbsp water
fresh cilantro, chopped

1. Using a spice grinder or a coffee grinder, grind together the coriander seeds, cloves, peppercorns, cinnamon stick, and cardamom pod.

2. Heat the oil in a sauté pan over medium heat and add the cumin seeds and stir until they are lightly toasted and fragrant.

3. Add the onion and garlic and cook until onions are lightly browned.

4. Add the turmeric and stir, then add the chili powder and salt, to taste.

5. Add the ground spices and minced ginger and stir.

6. Add the okra and 2 Tbsp of water and cook, uncovered, over low heat until okra is soft.

7. Garnish with fresh cilantro and serve with rice or naan.

TAAJ INDIAN CUISINE
128 WEST THIRD AVENUE

Banana Chocolate Chip Upside-Down Cake

Signature Tastes of SPOKANE

Topping:
⅓ C. + 2 Tbsp dark brown sugar, packed
2 Tbsp butter, cubed, softened
3–4 ripe medium bananas, sliced ¼-inch thick
a few drops of lemon juice

Cake:
1 ½ C. all-purpose flour
1 tsp baking powder
½ tsp baking soda
½ tsp salt
1 tsp ground cinnamon
¾ C. granulated sugar
2 Tbsp butter, melted
2 large eggs
1 C. banana puree (approximately 2 bananas)
⅓ C. sour cream
½ tsp vanilla extract
½ C. chocolate chips (bittersweet or semisweet)

1. Preheat the oven to 350ºF.

2. To make the topping, place the brown sugar and butter in an 8-inch square cake pan. Warm the pan directly on the stovetop over low heat, stirring just until the sugar is thoroughly moistened and bubbling. Remove from heat. (sugar will not be completely smooth). Cool to room temperature.

3. Arrange banana slices in slightly overlapping rows over the melted brown sugar. Sprinkle with a few drops of lemon juice.

4. For the cake, whisk together the flour, baking powder, baking soda, salt, and cinnamon in a large bowl, making sure there are no lumps. Mix in the granulated sugar.

5. In a small bowl, mix together the butter, eggs, banana puree, sour cream, and vanilla extract.

6. Make a well in the center of the dry ingredients and stir in the wet ingredients until almost combined. Do not over mix. Gently fold in the chocolate chips.

7. Scrape the batter into the pan over the banana topping, then use a spatula to carefully spread the batter evenly over the sliced bananas.

8. Bake for 40 minutes, or until the cake feels just set in the center when you touch it.

9. Cool the cake about 20 minutes, then run a knife along the edges of the cake to help release it from the pan. Place a serving platter over the cake pan and gently invert the cake on the platter. The cake is best served warm with whipped cream or vanilla ice cream the day it is made.

Taste Café
180 South Howard Street

"I like to keep things simple — really showcasing what is in season and letting the quality of the ingredients speak for themselves."
Hannah Heber, Co-owner and Pastry Chef

CHICKEN TIKKA MASALA

Signature Tastes of SPOKANE

Chicken Marinade:
2 lb. boneless, skinless chicken breast
½ C. plain yogurt
½ tsp salt
1 tsp garam masala
½ tsp chili powder

Sauce:
2 Tbsp oil
3 large onions, finely chopped
6–8 garlic cloves, chopped
1 (2-inch) piece of ginger, minced
2 tsp salt
1 tsp turmeric
1 tsp red chili powder
1 tsp ground cumin
2 Tbsp tomato sauce
2 oz. water
½ C. half and half
1 tsp dry fenugreek leaves

1. Mix yogurt, salt, garam masala, and chili powder in a bowl and stir well. Place chicken breasts in the marinade, and let sit for at least 8 hours (preferably 24) in the refrigerator.

2. Preheat oven to 350°F and bake chicken for 45–55 minutes. Remove chicken from oven and let cool, then cut into ¾-inch cubes and set aside.

3. Add the oil to a medium sauce pan and heat over medium high. Add the onions and sauté until soft and browned. Add the garlic and ginger and continue cooking for a few minutes, stirring occasionally.

4. Add the salt, turmeric, chili powder, and cumin and cook for a few minutes, then add the tomato sauce and approximately 2 oz. water.

5. Reduce heat, and using a hand blender, puree the mixture of onions and spices until smooth.

6. Add in the cubed chicken and the half and half and stir. Cook until the mixture is well blended and the chicken is heated through. Garnish with fenugreek leaves and enjoy with rice and naan.

TASTE OF INDIA
3110 NORTH DIVISION STREET

"As soon as I was old enough to drive, I got a job at a local newspaper. There was someone who influenced me. He wrote a column for The Guardian from this tiny village in India."
Nicholas D. Kristof

son

Polenta with Peperonata

We are Davide and Stephanie Trezzi and we live on our farm and work together at a variety of things we love to do. When we haven't been dry farming wine grapes, vegetables, and herbs, making wine, and catering, we've been pursuing the retail part of our business by cooking, packaging, and freezing some of our catering foods to sell on our farm and at a local farmers' market. In 2009 we converted our tractor barn into a tasting room and we opened up the farm to hosting events in 2010.

Peperonata:
olive oil
1 large yellow onion, sliced
5 whole garlic cloves
2 hot Italian sausages, cut into bite-size pieces
12 oz. steak, cut into bite-size pieces
splash of red wine
1 C. marinara sauce
2 yellow bell peppers, sliced
2 red bell peppers, sliced
2 orange bell peppers, sliced
1 C. water

Polenta:
3 qt. boiling water
2 tsp salt (or to taste)
3 C. medium ground polenta

Peperonata:

1. Heat olive oil in a large skillet over medium heat. Add onions and whole cloves of garlic and sauté for 3 minutes. Add sausage and steak, sauté for a few more minutes. Add a splash of red wine and the marinara sauce and stir, add peppers and 1 C. of water, stirring until all ingredients are incorporated. Cover, reduce heat, and simmer 40–50 minutes. Stir occasionally until peppers are very soft, sausage is cooked through, and liquid is reduced.

Polenta:

1. In a heavy sauce pan, bring the water and salt to a boil. Pour the polenta in slowly and whisk to smooth out any lumps. Reduce the heat and simmer, uncovered, for 20–30 minutes. Stir the polenta frequently; it is done when a spoon will stand up in the middle.

To Serve:

1. Scoop a generous amount of the soft, hot polenta onto a deep plate or large shallow bowl and spoon the hot peperonata with juices on top. Mangia!

Wine Pairing: Trezzi Farm Estate 2008 Barbera

Trezzi Farm, Food, & Wine
17700 North Dunn Road

"Simplicity is the ultimate sophistication."
Leonardo Da Vinci

Signature Taste of SPOKANE

Twigs Bistro has four locations conveniently located around the premier areas of Spokane. We are known for our thirty-six signature martinis and our eclectic menu which features regional American cuisine. We are open for lunch and dinner seven days a week and for breakfast on the weekends. Our signature Truffle Steak Penne has been a staple on our menu for years and is the most popular entrée that Twigs serves! Open a great bottle of Washington Cabernet and enjoy the truffle-flavored Alfredo sauce that accompanies the tender pieces of steak and broccolini.

2 oz. olive oil
1 lb. culotte steak
(or top sirloin), cut into
bite-size pieces
1 oz. garlic, minced
1 oz. shallots, minced
4 oz. cooked
bacon, chopped
½ lb. broccolini,
cut into 1-inch pieces
2 C. heavy cream
6 oz. parmesan
cheese, shredded
¾ oz. white truffle oil
salt and white pepper,
to taste
30 oz. cooked penne
pasta, drained

Garnish:
2 oz. parmesan
cheese, shaved
3 oz. diced tomato
2 Tbsp chopped
fresh parsley

1. Heat the oil in a large pan over medium-high heat and add the steak pieces, tossing occasionally until browned.

2. Add the garlic, shallots, bacon, and broccolini and heat through.

3. Add the heavy cream and bring to a boil, reduce heat and simmer, reduce the liquid by half, then add the shredded parmesan cheese and stir.

4. After cheese has melted completely, add the truffle oil and season to taste with salt and white pepper.

5. Add in the pre-cooked pasta, tossing to coat. Place into serving dishes, garnish with shaved parmesan, diced tomatoes, and chopped parsley. Enjoy!

TWIGS BISTRO & MARTINI BAR
MULTIPLE LOCATIONS

"There is nothing better than building a team of great people that serve the local community."
Trevor Blackwell, Director of Operations

ALASKAN
BREWING

Ugly Bettie's
Public House

THIS WEEK
JACK DANIEL'S

Happy Hour 4-6 Daily!
Sundays - FREE POOL 6pm-9pm
Tues/Wed - Pitcher of PBR/PABST $7pm
Thursdays - Nena Live on the Patio 6-8
Tommy G's Live Tuesday-Sat 8:30pm
Fridays - 6/15 Village Blues
UB Tiki Bar Open

Caramelized Onion and Asparagus Quesadilla

Signature Tastes of SPOKANE

½ C. unsalted butter
4 large onions,
thinly sliced
6 stalks of asparagus
large flour tortillas
shredded cheddar cheese

1. Melt butter in a shallow frying pan and add the onions, stir to lightly coat the onions with butter. Caramelize onions over medium-low heat, stirring often, approximately 45 minutes.

2. Meanwhile, trim off the woody ends of the asparagus and cut into ¼-inch pieces.

3. When the onions are caramelized, add the asparagus and steam until crisp, about 2 minutes.

4. Heat a large flat pan over high heat and lightly crisp one side of a tortilla then flip it over. Add the shredded cheese and caramelized onion mixture to one half of the tortilla then fold in half and cook until the cheese is melted. Cut quesadilla into slices and serve with sour cream, salsa, or ranch.

UGLY BETTIE'S PUBLIC HOUSE
211 NORTH DIVISION STREET

"A woman who cannot be ugly is not beautiful."
Karl Kraus

Residing on a cozy corner of the South Hill, Vin Rouge delivers Northwest bistro-style fare in a warm atmosphere. Owner Jeff Jenkins's hand-picked wine list is an eclectic mix of wines from around the world, with an emphasis on some of the Northwest's best small production wineries. Chef Jae Best brings a wealth of experience from award-winning restaurants in the Northwest and region. The style of the menu, designed to complement the wine, is natural with a focus on local products from small farms.

1 lb. sashimi grade tuna, cut into ⅜-inch dice
1 Tbsp sesame oil
2 Tbsp soy sauce
2 Tbsp honey
1 tsp fresh ginger, peeled and finely minced
2 Tbsp fresh lemon juice
1 Tbsp red onion, finely diced
1 tsp Italian parsley, finely chopped
pinch of fleur de sel or coarse sea salt

1. To make the sauce, whisk together the sesame oil, soy sauce, honey, ginger, lemon juice, red onion, parsley, and salt.

2. Toss tuna with sauce.

3. Press into 4-oz. molds (such as a ramekin or custard cup), invert onto serving plates.

4. Garnish with more fleur de sel and garnish. Serve with crisp crackers.

3029 EAST TWENTY-NINTH AVENUE

VIN ROUGE

"There is no good life without good food and good wine."
Jae Best, Chef

SOUTHWEST CHILI DIP

Our goal is to provide you with a unique selection of delightful wines and deli-
cious food for a truly wonderful dining experience. Our welcoming and atten-
tive staff and elegant décor will make you feel like you are indulging yourself.
We hope that you will discover exciting new flavors as well as tasty favorites
to make Vintages at 611 your special destination on Spokane's South Hill.

2 C. shredded Mexican
cheese
1 C. mayonnaise
1 Tbsp Tabasco
½ tsp garlic salt
⅔ C. diced green chilies
1 C. sliced black olives,
divided
½ C. diced tomatoes
¼ C. diced scallions

1. Preheat oven to 350°F.

2. In a bowl, mix together the shredded cheese, mayonnaise, Tabasco, and garlic salt.

3. Stir in the diced chilies and ½ C. of the sliced black
olives.

4. Place dip into small baking dish and bake for 20 minutes until bubbling.

5. Garnish with diced tomatoes, ½ C. of sliced olives,
and ¼ C. diced scallions. Serve with tortilla chips.

VINTAGES AT 611
611 EAST TWENTY-NINTH AVENUE

"Vintages at 611 is known for its fabulous food, classic cocktails,
and our award-winning wine list."
Tana Rekofke, Owner

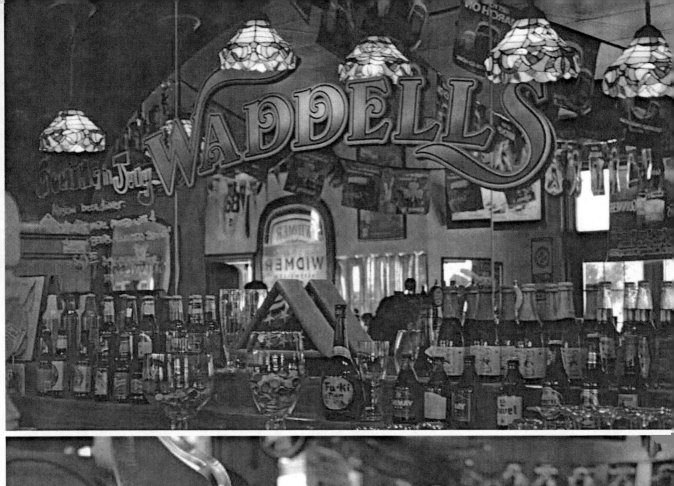

OATMEAL STOUT STEW

Signature Tastes of SPOKANE

Waddell's Pub & Grille is located on the South Hill of Spokane. We are proud to have the largest draft selection in town with thirty-five handles. Along with the outstanding beer, our food is also making a name for itself — the best burgers in town, Reuben sandwiches, hand-dipped fish-n-chips, and the list goes on. Waddell's has been featured on the Food Network's Diners, Drive-Ins, and Dives and we invite you to come and try some of our mouthwatering specials. If watching the big game is what you're after we have plenty of TV's and a great patio to enjoy the sun!

Sachet d'épices:
1 8x8-inch piece of cheesecloth
1 cinnamon stick
3 whole cloves
6 whole black peppercorns
2 bay leaves
2 fresh sprigs of thyme

Stew:
4 slices of bacon, finely chopped
1 (2-lb.) flank steak or brisket, cut into ½-inch cubes
¼ C. tomato paste
¾ C. all-purpose flour
11 C. beef broth, warmed
3 C. of stout beer, at room temperature
4 C. baby red potatoes, ½-inch dice
4 medium carrots, ½-inch dice
1 large white onion, ½-inch dice
3 stalks of celery, ½-inch dice
2 C. fresh sugar peas (or frozen)
4 garlic cloves, minced
2 Tbsp sugar
1 tsp red pepper flakes
Tabasco sauce, to taste (optional)
salt and pepper, to taste
2 C. grated havarti cheese

1. Place all the spices in the center of the cheesecloth and fold up to make a small pouch, twist and tie with a piece of butchers twine long enough to tie around the sachet and then to the handle of the pot. Set aside.
2. Cook the bacon in an 8-qt. stew pot over medium heat until crispy, stirring often, about 5 to 6 minutes.
3. Add the beef and cook, stirring often, about 25 minutes. Add tomato paste and cook for 2 minutes. Add the flour to make a roux and cook for 5 minutes, stirring constantly.
4. Slowly add the beef broth to the roux, stirring constantly, turn the heat to low and cook for about 10 minutes to cook off the starch in the flour.
5. Add the beer and simmer for 20 minutes.
6. Add the red potatoes and cook for 5 minutes. Add the carrots, cook for 5 minutes. Add the onion, cook for 5 minutes. Add the celery, cook for 5 minutes, and add the fresh peas, cook for 5 minutes (if using frozen peas, add at the end of cooking). Finally, add the minced garlic.
7. Place the sachet d'épices into the pot and tie the twine to the handle of the pot. Simmer the stew uncovered, for 30–45 minutes, until all vegetables and meat are tender and stew is thickened. (Add the frozen peas at this point, if using.)
8. Season the stew with the sugar, red pepper flakes, Tabasco sauce (optional), and salt and pepper. Ladle stew into bowls, sprinkle with grated havarti cheese and serve with warm rustic bread. Cheers!

WADDELL'S PUB & GRILLE
4318 SOUTH REGAL STREET

"Our customers are the greatest! Thank you for making Waddell's Pub & Grille part of the neighborhood. Go Zags!"
Michael Noble, Chef

BELGIAN WAFFLES

Signature Tastes of SPOKANE

Waffles Plus is a charming and cozy diner where all of our customers are treated like old friends. The idea behind the food was inspired by owner Dale Westhaver's kids — which is why waffles come topped with every imaginable candy, fruit, ice cream, signature syrup, and of course, mounds of whipped cream. The great food and relaxing atmosphere make Waffles Plus Spokane's ultimate hidden gem.

3¼ C. waffle flour, sifted
1½ C. water
½ C. buttermilk
2 eggs, beaten
3 Tbsp melted butter
2 tsp vanilla extract

1. Preheat waffle iron to 350°F.

2. Place sifted waffle flour in a large bowl and set aside. In a separate bowl, combine water, buttermilk, eggs, melted butter, and vanilla extract and mix well. Add the wet ingredients to the large bowl with the waffle flour and whip until batter is smooth — no lumps! Leave at room temperature for 30 minutes.

3. Pour batter into pre-heated waffle iron and cook approximately 3 minutes, or until golden brown. (Time will vary depending on size of waffle iron).

4. Remove waffles and serve with any or all of the following toppings: strawberries, bananas, blueberries, peaches, apple or cherry pie filling (pre-warmed), ice cream, chocolate candies, or pecans. For traditional waffles, serve with butter and maple syrup or flavored syrup such as blueberry, apricot, or strawberry. Add pre-cooked ham, bacon, or sausage to the waffle batter for a delicious savory treat!

WAFFLES PLUS
2625 NORTH MONROE STREET

"Don't forget the whipped cream!"
Dale Westhaver, Owner

POBLANO-ARTICHOKE DIP WITH BLUE CORN CRACKERS

Wild Sage is Spokane's premier downtown bistro for casual and romantic dinners or for drinks, desserts, and small plates after an evening show or event. The restaurant is located in the core of the city's flourishing arts and entertainment venues, including the Fox and Bing Crosby theatres. The award-winning cuisine favors simple, whole foods creatively prepared with surprising blends of color, texture, and flavor. Returning guests anticipate the elegant artistry of each plate as much as the exquisite fare.

Blue Corn Crackers:
¾ C. all-purpose flour
½ C. blue cornmeal
1½ tsp salt
1½ tsp sugar
1 tsp ground cumin
1 tsp paprika
1 tsp chili powder
1 tsp baking soda
3 Tbsp + 1 tsp unsalted butter, cubed
¼ C. + 3 Tbsp cold water

Poblano-Artichoke Dip:
1 poblano chili
1 C. marinated artichoke hearts, drained
¼ C. sour cream
1 (8-oz.) package of cream cheese, softened
1 tsp garlic, chopped
¼ C. mayonnaise
¼ C. grated parmesan cheese
1 tsp finely chopped jalapeño
¼ C. scallions, finely chopped
¼ C. cilantro, finely chopped
pinch of salt and pepper
1 C. shredded Manchego cheese

Blue Corn Crackers:
1. Preheat oven to 275°F (250°F for convection oven).
2. Combine all the dry ingredients in a bowl. Add the butter and blend with a pastry cutter or by hand until butter is well incorporated. Add the cold water and gently mix (the batter will be slightly sticky). Turn onto a floured surface and fold together until the dough forms a ball. Allow to rest at room temperature for 10 minutes.
3. Divide dough in half. Place each half on a baking sheet lined with floured parchment paper. Roll dough out to fit the baking sheet, adding flour when needed to assist in rolling. Bake as is or cut into desired shape with a pizza wheel or knife. Bake for 20–25 minutes. Crackers will curl up slightly in center when done. Let cool.

Poblano-Artichoke Dip:
1. Roast the poblano chili over high heat of a grill until charred on the outside, place in a bowl and cover with plastic wrap for 15 minutes. Remove skin and seeds, finely chop.
2. Place all the ingredients except Manchego cheese into a mixing bowl and stir until thoroughly incorporated.
3. Place the dip in a medium sauce pan and heat slowly over medium-low heat. Melt shredded Manchego cheese over the top and serve with the blue corn crackers.

"At Wild Sage, our award-winning concept featuring fresh, locally grown and Northwest inspired cuisine will make you want to come back again and again. We update our menu frequently and are constantly in search of unique ingredients and flavors."
Charlie Connor, Executive Chef

A look...

...in the cupboard...

PORK CHOP POTATO BAKE

Bud Nameck is the announcer for Washington State University Cougar Basketball and reports from the sidelines during WSU football games. He's been the voice of Cougars on the hardwood since 1993. For his longtime work with the Cougars, Bud was recently awarded an honorary degree from WSU. Bud came to KXLY in 1982, after serving as Sports Information Director for Gonzaga University. He spent 13 years as KXLY Sports Director and has also been Program Director and morning news anchor of KXLY 920, and Program Director and talk show host for ESPN Radio AM 700, "The Ticket." Among his professional accomplishments, Bud has won an Emmy and has twice been named the Washington State Sportscaster of the Year. Sports has always played an important role in the San Francisco Bay area native's life. He played 3rd base for Santa Clara University before coming to the Northwest. Bud, his wife and daughter are proud to call Spokane home.

1–2 Tbsp oil
4–6 pork chops, ½-inch to ¾-inch thick
salt and pepper, to taste
½ C. sour cream
½ C. milk
24 oz. shredded potatoes, thawed if frozen
1 (10½-oz.) can cream of celery soup
1 C. grated cheddar cheese, divided
1 (6-oz.) can French fried onions, divided

1. Preheat oven to 350°F.

2. Heat the oil in a large sauté pan over medium-high heat. Brown the pork chops and season with salt and pepper to taste.

3. In a large bowl, mix the shredded potatoes, sour cream, milk, and cream of celery soup together. Stir in half of the cheddar cheese and half of the French fried onions.

4. Spray a large rectangular glass baking dish with non-stick spray and spoon the shredded potato mixture into the baking dish. Place the pork chops on top of the potatoes. Sprinkle the remaining cheese and onions on top.

5. Bake, uncovered, for 1 hour. Serve a portion of the potato mix along with a pork chop, a veggie of choice, and a salad and you have a dinner to enjoy!

Signature Tastes of SPOKANE

BROADCASTER, COUGAR SPORTS RADIO NETWORK

BUD NAMECK

"This Pork Chop Potato Bake is an easy casserole to prepare for a fall or winter evening meal."
Bud Nameck

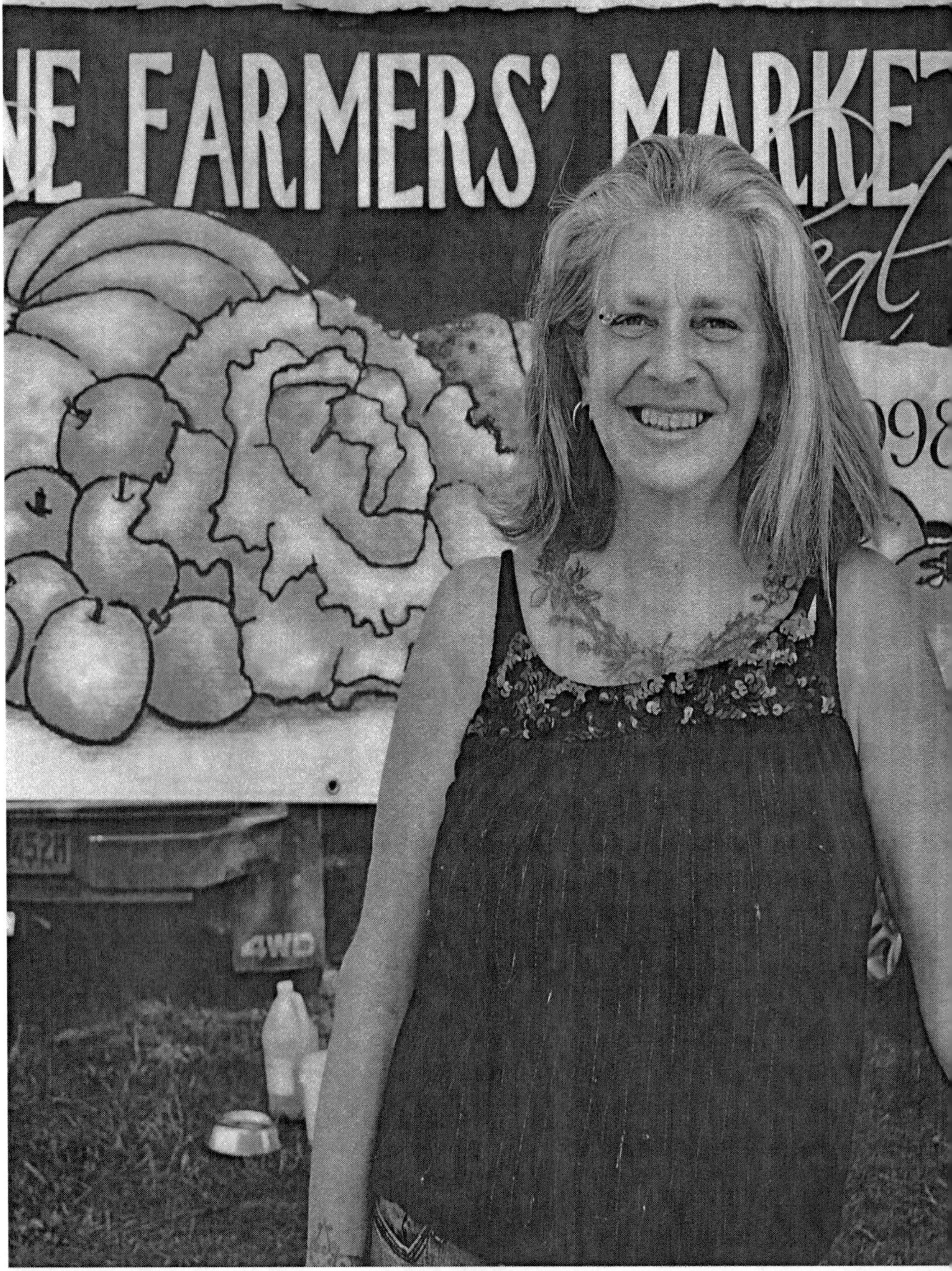
NE FARMERS' MARKE
4WD

BAKED PEARS WITH CASHEW CRÈME

Signature Tastes of SPOKANE

5 pears
2 Tbsp maple syrup
4 Tbsp lemon juice,
divided
1 ⅓ C. water
5 Tbsp raw
cashew pieces
¼ tsp salt
⅔ C. maple syrup
1½ Tbsp corn starch or
wheat starch
¼ C. unbleached white
flour
1½ tsp vanilla extract

1. Preheat oven to 350°F.

2. Cut pears in half lengthwise and core. Place cut-side down in a single layer in a glass baking dish. Mix 2 Tbsp maple syrup and 2 Tbsp lemon juice and pour over pears. Bake for approximately 30 minutes until tender.

3. Make the cashew crème by blending the water, cashew pieces, and salt together in a blender until very smooth. Add the maple syrup, corn starch, flour (use only 2 Tbsp for a thinner cream), and the 2 Tbsp remaining lemon juice and blend until very smooth.

4. Pour into a heavy-bottomed medium sauce pan and stir constantly over medium-high heat until the mixture is thick. Simmer over low heat for 1 minute. Remove from the heat and whisk in the vanilla extract. Spoon the crème onto baked pears.

DIRECTOR, SPOKANE FARMERS' MARKET, 10 WEST 5TH AVENUE

DIANE REUTER

"It is, in my view, the duty of an apple to be crisp and crunchable, but a pear should have such a texture as leads to silent consumption."
Edward Bunyard, 'The Anatomy of Dessert'

TENDERLOIN OF BEEF WITH MERLOT SAUCE

Founded in a garage by Greg Lipsker and Michael White, two attorney/winemakers, Barrister Winery is now located in a 100-year-old brick building in the historic Davenport Arts District in downtown Spokane. In the fall of 1997, we bought a 5-gallon home-winemaking kit on a whim while vacationing with our families. Since then, winemaking has become the "little hobby" that got out of control. In 2001, we took the quantum leap from home winemaking to becoming a bonded winery. Initially producing only red wine, we have ventured into small quantities of white, but reds are our specialty. Our grapes come from some of Washington's most prestigious vineyards (and a couple of sleepers). Our grapes are all hand picked, fermented in small lots and barrel-aged in French and American Oak for 16 to 36 months.

Beef Tenderloin:
1 (5-lb.) beef tenderloin roast, fat and silver skin removed
½ C. clarified butter
3 oz. cognac
1 Tbsp butter

Merlot Sauce:
1 shallot, chopped
1½ Tbsp butter
½ C. Barrister Red Mountain Merlot
1 C. beef stock
1 Tbsp corn starch, mixed with ¼ C. Merlot, stock, or water
⅓ C. tomato sauce
salt and pepper, to taste
¼ C. water, wine, or beef stock
1 Tbsp butter

Beef Tenderloin:

1. Preheat oven to 350°F.

2. Coat the tenderloin on all sides with the clarified butter and place on a rack in a roasting pan and bake for 45 minutes, turning once.

3. Remove roasting pan from the oven, pour cognac over beef and carefully ignite with a match. When the flame burns out, place the tenderloin on serving platter and cover with foil. Let meat rest at least 20 minutes before slicing.

4. Set roasting pan aside as you will need it to finish the merlot sauce.

Merlot Sauce:

1. In a medium pan, melt the butter over medium heat and add the shallots. Sauté shallots until soft, then add the merlot and cook until liquid is reduced by three-fourths. Add the beef stock and bring to a boil. Stir in corn starch mixture, tomato sauce, and season to taste with salt and pepper.

2. In the roasting pan, add ¼ C. water, wine, or broth and cook over medium heat, scraping brown bits from bottom of pan. Add the merlot sauce, simmer and reduce slightly, then remove from heat and stir in 1 Tbsp butter. Pour a bit of the sauce over the roast and serve remaining sauce separately.

Wine Pairing: Barrister Red Mountain Merlot.

GREG LIPSKER AND MICHAEL WHITE

WINEMAKERS, BARRISTER WINERY, 1213 WEST RAILROAD AVENUE

"Being passionate about our wine, we try to make wine in the style we like to drink. We are striving to produce only premium quality wines. Although it is a business now, it is still a labor of love."
Greg Lipsker and Michael White

Seared Scallops with Glazed Chorizo Sausage and Tomato-Leek Confit and the Perfect Party Gin and Tonic

Jess Walter is the author of five novels and one nonfiction book. His work has been translated into more than 20 languages and his essays, short fiction, criticism and journalism have been widely published. Jess Walter's sixth novel, "Beautiful Ruins" is set for release in spring of 2012. He is also the author of "The Financial Lives of the Poets," 2009, "The Zero," a 2006 National Book Award finalist and "Citizen Vince," winner of the 2005 Edgar Award Allan Poe for best novel. Walter lives with his wife and children in his childhood home of Spokane, Washington.

Signature Tastes of SPOKANE

Scallop Dish:
Order out. I have no idea how to make this.

Gin and Tonics:
20 gallons of plastic-bottled gin
32 gallons of tonic
12 limes
6 bags of ice
1 kiddie pool
1 snorkel

Gin and Tonics:

Mix gin and tonic in pool. Slice limes. Drop limes and ice in gin mixture. Stir with your kid's T-ball bat. Send your kids to your sister's house for the weekend. Not the sister under house arrest for stealing your grandmother's pain medication, the other one. Ask someone you trust to hide your car keys. Call in sick for work. Do not operate machinery or make any important financial decisions for a while. Do not call your old girlfriend for the CDs she stole, or the old boss who twice caught you sleeping under your desk without your pants on. If you do call your old boss, remember that he has Caller ID, and that yelling, "You've never heard of a three-strike policy, ass-face?" is not likely to sway him at this late date. Do not invite over that creepy neighbor who always weed-whacks without his shirt on and makes "jokes" about how he and his wife are swingers. On day six, when you find the remnants of a fancy scallop dish in what's left of your kitchen, pretend that you remember ordering it.

Serves 80

Jess Walter
Spokane Author

"When her guests were awash with champagne and with gin,
She was recklessly sober, as sharp as a pin.
An abstemious man would reel at her look,
As she rolled a bright eye and praised his last book."
William Plomer

Basil

nderson's

Farm Fresh P

grown in Stevens C

From O

PICKED

CO

WATERMELON SALAD WITH RASPBERRY-MINT VINAIGRETTE

DIRECTOR, SOUTH PERRY FARMERS' MARKET, 915-924 SOUTH PERRY STREET

MARYANN DELANEY

I love to make this Watermelon Salad with Raspberry-Mint Vinaigrette in the summer when the raspberries are just coming on and watermelon is aplenty at South Perry Farmers' Market. I can find all of the ingredients for this salad locally and it is as refreshing and delicious as it is beautiful.
The South Perry Farmers' Market is every Thursday from 3-6 pm at 924 South Perry Street, and indoors across the street during the winter.

Raspberry-Mint Syrup:
1 C. raspberries
2 Tbsp sugar
¼ C. mint leaves

Dressing:
¼ C. raspberry-mint syrup
½ C. olive oil
¼ C. white balsamic vinegar
1 tsp fresh lemon juice
salt and pepper, to taste

Salad:
5 C. (seedless) watermelon, cut into medium-to-large wedges
1 large red onion, cut into ¼-inch slices
1 medium bunch of watercress (may substitute arugula)
1 C. fresh raspberries
¼ C. mint leaves
4 oz. chèvre, crumbled

1. Make the raspberry-mint syrup by pureeing the raspberries, sugar, and mint leaves together and strain in a fine-mesh sieve. Reserve a ¼ C. for the salad dressing.

2. Make the dressing by whisking together the raspberry-mint syrup, olive oil, white balsamic vinegar, lemon juice, and season to taste with salt and pepper.

3. Marinate the red onion in the dressing for 20 minutes.

4. Lay the watercress on a large platter and layer some of the marinated onions on top of it. Continue by layering the watermelon, raspberries, mint leaves, and then top the salad with remaining onions and dressing. Garnish generously with raspberries, mint, and chèvre.

Signature Tastes of SPOKANE

"The Farmers' Market is the slowly turning Lazy Susan of the seasons."
John Hollander

Onion Soup

Mary Verner was the 43rd Mayor of the City of Spokane. While completing her Master's Degree, Mary was offered a position in Natural Resources Management with the Spokane Tribe of Indians. Mary moved to the Spokane area in 1992, and immediately immersed herself in her community as an active citizen and volunteer. She attended Gonzaga Law School while working full-time, and achieved her law degree in 1999. Mary likes to spend her free time with family, friends, and neighbors enjoying the Spokane area's beautiful natural environment.

Onion Soup:
1 large yellow onion,
cut into large chunks
water or vegetable broth
any or all of the
following spices to taste:
cayenne pepper
curry powder
chili powder
ginger
dash of
Worcestershire sauce

Homemade Croutons:
sliced whole-wheat
bread
butter
salt and pepper, to taste
grated mild cheese
for topping

1. Put the onion in large sauce pan and cover with water or vegetable broth.

2. Add a little bit of everything spicy in the spice cabinet, such as a dash of cayenne pepper, dash of curry powder, dash of ginger, dash of chili powder—whatever sounds good. Add salt and pepper to taste, then add a generous dollop of Worcestershire sauce.

3. Bring the soup to a boil, then turn down the heat and let simmer until onions are thoroughly tender.

4. Meanwhile, prepare homemade croutons by toasting wheat bread with butter, salt, and pepper and cut the toast into crouton-sized pieces.

5. Grate some of the mild cheeses in your cheese drawer—cheddar, Muenster, Monterey jack, mozzarella, parmesan, Romano, whatever you have.

6. When ready to serve, scoop the onion soup into large soup bowls, add croutons and cheese, and enjoy! If soup bowls can be put in the oven, an extra touch is to place the bowls under the broiler for a few seconds to sizzle the cheeses just before serving.

MARY VERNER
SPOKANE CITIZEN

"Onion soup sustains. The process of making it is somewhat like the process of learning to love. It requires commitment, extraordinary effort, time, and will make you cry."
Ronni Lundy

ARROZ CON GANDULES

Mike Gonzalez is news anchor at KXLY 4 TV and the founder of the Hispanic Food Network which was launched in 2010. Mike is also the host of HFNTV's show In the Kitchen ("En La Cocina") which features Latin cooking and culture in the Northwest. Born in Miami, Mike comes to Spokane from news stations in Nebraska, Missouri, and North Carolina. To keep up with Mike as he profiles local businesses, people, and the stories behind the food visit www.hispanicfoodnetwork.com and www.hfntv.com

Signature Tastes of **SPOKANE**

3 Tbsp olive oil
4 Tbsp sofrito
(jarred or make your own by dicing onion, bell pepper (any kind), garlic, cilantro, and tomato)
¼ C. chopped bacon
¼ C. chopped ham or sausage
5 C. water
1 (15-oz) can green or dry pigeon peas, drained
2 Tbsp Spanish olives
½ tsp tomato paste
½ tsp ground oregano
½ tsp ground cumin
2 bay leaves
1 envelope sazón with annato
salt and black pepper, to taste
2 ½ C. long-grain white rice

1. Heat the oil in a pot over high heat. When the oil is hot, add the bacon. When the bacon is cooked but not crisp, add the ham or sausage. Once browned, add the sofrito. Stir fry for about 1 minute.

2. Next add the water, peas, olives, tomato paste, oregano, cumin, bay leaves, and the envelope of sazón. Add salt and pepper to taste.

3. Bring mixture to a boil then stir in the rice. Once it has begun to boil again, lower the heat, stir once, then cover with a tight fitting lid. Let simmer for about 30–40 minutes on low heat, stirring occasionally (once about every 10 minutes) until the rice is tender.

MIKE GONZALEZ
NEWS ANCHOR, KXLY-TV

"This Arroz con Gandules is a traditional Puerto Rican Dish that I grew up with."
Mike Gonzales

Gordon and Marilyn Beck started farming what is now Beck's Harvest House and Orchard in 1987, purchasing the land 1989. We started selling fresh u-pick and picked fruits, country gifts, homemade pies and ice cream. The business grew slow at first, but through hard work and perseverance by the Beck's, growth continued throughout the years. In 1996 the business had finally outgrown the small 100-year-old barn on the property. That's when we started the project of building what is now the current Harvest House. Today the building hosts a gift shop filled with unique gift ideas as well as gourmet food items, a wine shop stocked with excellent wines from down the road to around the world and unique fruit wines and beers, a kitchen where pies, turnovers, rolls, doughnuts and other goodies are prepared daily. We built patios and decks for our customers to enjoy their lunch, an ice-cream cone, a bottle of wine or special events where they have a view over looking the orchard and Mt. Spokane, and of course a bounty of fresh quality fruits and vegetables.

1 egg
1 C. sour cream,
room temperature
¾ C. sugar
2 Tbsp all-purpose flour
¼ tsp vanilla extract
dash of salt
2¼ C. finely chopped,
peeled baking apples (2–3)
¼ tsp grated lemon zest
1 unbaked pie crust

Crumb Topping:
½ C. sugar
⅓ C. all-purpose flour
¾ tsp. cinnamon
¼ C. unsalted butter,
softened

1. Preheat oven to 450°F.

2. Beat the egg in a large bowl then blend in sour cream, sugar, flour, vanilla extract, and salt. Fold in the apples and lemon zest. Pour into pie crust and bake for 10 minutes. Reduce oven temperature to 350°F and bake 30 minutes, or until crust is golden brown.

3. Meanwhile, prepare crumb topping. Put sugar, flour, and cinnamon in a bowl and cut in the butter until well incorporated. Sprinkle topping over pie and bake for an additional 15 minutes. Serve warm or cool.

MANAGER, HARVEST HOUSE, 9919 EAST GREENBLUFF ROAD

TODD BECK

"This French Apple Pie is apple pie with the à la mode built in. Delicious!"
Todd Beck, Manager

SPICY SPAGHETTI

Josh is the owner of Nectar Tasting Room, a modern wine tasting space shared by five Washington wineries in downtown Spokane. Josh also publishes Spokane Wine Magazine and has a consulting company that helps businesses navigate the waters of social media and relationship marketing. Nectar Tasting Room was recently selected by the readers of Inland Business Catalyst Magazine as the top start up of 2011. Readers also selected Josh as one of the 20 under 40 business people in Spokane. Josh's website is one of the most read wine blogs in the country and was recently highlighted on MSNBC.com. In his spare time, Josh is the wine consulting co-host of HFNTV's In the Kitchen with Mike Gonzalez and also enjoys playing guitar and just hanging out with friends.

1 lb. lean ground beef
½ lb. Italian sausage, casings removed, crumbled
fresh chopped oregano, to taste
fresh chopped basil, to taste
dash of garlic salt
1 (24-oz.) jar of spaghetti sauce
1 (6-oz.) can tomato paste
1 (15-oz.) can diced tomatoes with green chilies
1 jalapeño pepper, diced
3–4 garlic cloves, minced
½ of 1 onion, diced
spaghetti, cooked and drained

1. In a large pan, brown the ground beef and Italian sausage over medium heat, stirring frequently. Add some fresh chopped oregano, fresh chopped basil, and a dash of garlic salt, to taste. Drain off the excess fat from the pan.

2. In a large pot, add the jar of spaghetti sauce, tomato paste, diced tomatoes, jalapeño, garlic, onion. Add fresh chopped oregano and fresh chopped basil, to taste. Bring to a slow simmer over medium heat; add the meat and simmer for a few minutes to blend the flavors. Spoon the sauce over the spaghetti as desired.

Wine Pairing: I enjoy this dish with fresh garlic bread and a simple green salad with a balsamic vinegar dressing. Since the spaghetti sauce and balsamic vinegar are both fairly acidic, a great wine pairing is Barbera, Primitivo, or a nice Sangiovese. Stop by Nectar Tasting Room, we've got some of each.

OWNER, NECTAR TASTING ROOM, 120 NORTH STEVENS

JOSH WADE

"We were created for relationships, both horizontal and vertical. Grow and nurture them both and you will live a blessed life."
Josh Wade

CHIPOTLE CHICKEN TORTILLA SOUP

Signature Taste of SPOKANE

1 rotisserie-style chicken
1 Tbsp extra virgin olive oil
1 onion, finely chopped, reserve 3 Tbsp for garnish
4 garlic cloves, minced
3 C. chicken stock
1 chipotle in adobo, chopped + 2 Tbsp sauce
1 (15-oz.) can of black beans, rinsed
½ C. of sliced black olives
1 C. frozen corn
salt, to taste
2–4 oz. of tequila
juice of 1 lime
½ C. chopped cilantro, plus more for garnish
1 (28-oz.) can crushed fire-roasted tomatoes
4 C. lightly crushed corn tortilla chips
2 C. shredded Mexican-style cheese
1 lime, cut into wedges

1. Pull all the meat off the rotisserie chicken and set aside. Discard skin.

2. Heat olive oil in large pot over medium heat and add the onions and garlic and cook for 5 minutes. Add the chicken stock, chicken meat, chopped chipotle and sauce, black beans, black olives, corn, salt to taste, tequila, lime juice, chopped cilantro, and the tomatoes. Bring to a boil, then simmer for 20 minutes.

3. Fill bowls with the soup and place a pile of crushed tortilla chips on top. Cover liberally with cheese. Serve with lime wedges, cilantro, and more onions as desired.

MARGARET CROOM
CREATOR AND PUBLISHER OF NOSEY PARKER®

Braised Short Ribs with Arbor Crest Dionysus

Kristina Mielke-van Löben Sels and Jim van Löben Sels

Arbor Crest Wine Cellars, 4705 North Fruit Hill Road

Signature Tastes of SPOKANE

In 1982, the Mielke family started Arbor Crest Wine Cellars, a venture that would eventually grow into the Inland Northwest's premier winery. In 1999 Kristina Mielke-van Löben Sels came from her position in Sonoma County, California, to take over as the head winemaker for Arbor Crest, along with her husband Jim van Löben Sels, now the current manager. More than forty years after the original van Löben Sels release in California, Jim, Kristina, and their three children are carrying on the traditions of their families and the industry with the re-introduction the van Löben Sels label.

6 bone-in short ribs
kosher salt
olive oil
1 large onion, roughly chopped
2 stalks of celery, roughly chopped
2 carrots, peeled, roughly chopped
2 garlic cloves, smashed
1½ C. tomato paste
4 tsp Worcestershire sauce
2 Tbsp brown sugar
2–3 C. Arbor Crest Dionysus
½ C. of dried cherries
2 C. water
1 bunch of fresh thyme
2 bay leaves

1. Preheat oven to 375°F.

2. Season the short ribs generously with kosher salt. Coat the bottom of a large oven-proof pot with olive oil and set over high heat. When the oil is hot, but not smoking, add a few short ribs to the pot at a time and brown very well, about 2–3 minutes per side. Set aside browned ribs in a bowl, discard the oil in the pot, and wipe out the pot with paper towels.

3. Puree all the vegetables and garlic in a food processor until a thick paste forms. Season generously with salt. Using the same pot, add the pureed vegetables and cook over medium-high heat until mixture is dark and a crust has formed on the bottom of the pot, approximately 5–7 minutes. Scrape up the crust with a spatula and cook until crust reforms. Scrape the crust again and add the tomato paste and cook for 1–2 minutes. Scrape again and add the Worcestershire sauce and brown sugar and cook for 4–5 more minutes. Add the Arbor Crest Dionysus and the dried cherries and scrape the bottom of the pot. Reduce the mixture by half; be careful not to burn.

4. Return the short ribs and their juices to the pot and add enough water to just cover the meat, approximately 2 cups. Add the bunch of thyme and bay leaves. Cover the pot and place in the oven to braise for 3 hours. Check periodically during cooking and add more water to the pot if ribs seem dry. Turn the ribs over halfway through cooking time and remove the lid during the last 20 minutes of cooking to brown the meat and to reduce the sauce. Serve the short ribs with the braising sauce over mashed potatoes or creamy polenta.

Wine Pairing: Arbor Crest Dionysus, Meritage Red Blend

"Arbor Crest wines are ones that showcase the varietals and the region in which they are grown, most importantly the vineyard site. It is my aspiration to make the best possible wines using traditional methods and utilizing the latest technologies with superior Washington State fruit. We are excited to present you with our wines, from our family, to yours. Cheers!"
Kristina Mielke-van Löben Sels, Winemaker

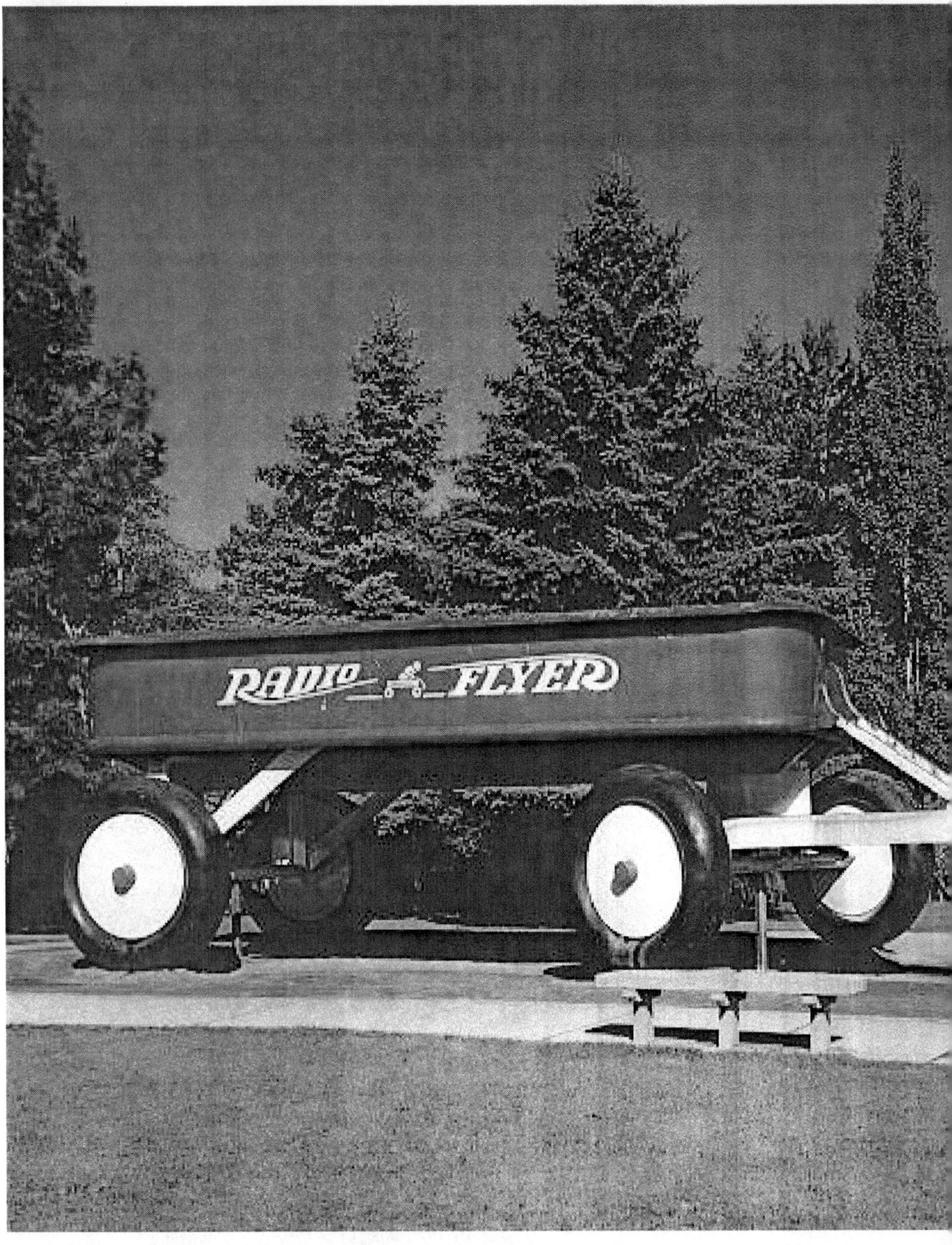
RADIO FLYER

INDEX O' RECIPES

"I should have no objection to go over the same life from its beginning to the end: requesting only the advantage authors have, of correcting in a second edition the faults of the first."

Benjamin Franklin

Steven W. Siler is a firefighter-cum-chef serving in Bellingham, Washington. Long marinated in the epicurean heritage of the Deep South, Steven has spent over 20 years (dear God has it been that long?!) in the much-vaulted restaurant industry from BOH to FOH to chef. In addition, he has served as an editor and contributing writer for several food publications. When not trying to shove food down his fellow firefighters' gullets, he enjoys sailing and sampling the finest of scotches and wines, and has an irrational love affair with opera. He swears one day he will relive the above picture on the Gulf Coast with a good Will.

Nicole L. Manganaro is a freelance editor specializing in cookbooks and regional guidebooks. As an adventurous eater and home cook she has enjoyed exploring the exciting food scene in Spokane, and as a result of working on this book, she was pleased to discover a few more hidden gems. Nicole and her husband Marc are the proud parents of twin sons, John and Michael, born shortly after they relocated to Spokane in 2007. She also has her three step-children, Anthony, Thomas, and Rania, to thank for their willingness to eat many of her culinary experiments. Prior to moving to Spokane, she was a production editor at Rutgers University Press in New Jersey. This is her first book.

CPSIA information can be obtained at www.ICGtesting.com
Printed in the USA
LVOW11s1539150714

394459LV00009B/607/P